WHAT A WORLD 2

READING

SECOND EDITION

Amazing Stories
from Around the Globe

Milada Broukal

PEARSON
Longman

What a World Reading 2: Amazing Stories from Around the Globe

Pearson Education, 10 Bank Street, White Plains, NY 10606

Staff credits: The people who made up the *What a World Reading 2* team, representing editorial, production, design, and manufacturing, are Pietro Alongi, Rhea Banker, John Barnes, John Brezinsky, Aerin Csigay, Nancy Flaggman, Christopher Leonowicz, Amy McCormick, Linda Moser, Robert Ruvo, Jennifer Stem, and Patricia Wosczyk.
Cover and text design: Patricia Wosczyk
Text composition: ElectraGraphics, Inc.
Text font: Minion
Photo Credits: Cover, Kenneth Garrett/National Geographic Creative/Getty Images; Page 1, The Art Archive/Musée des Beaux Arts Grenoble/Gianni Dagli Orti; p. 8, Gio Mere/Alamy; p. 15, Narendra Shrestha/epa/Corbis; p. 22, Shutterstock.com; p. 29, Time & Life Pictures/Getty Images; p. 36, Kit Kittle/Corbis; p. 43, Shutterstock.com; p. 50, The Art Archive/Pasteur birthplace Dole/Alfredo Dagli Orti; p. 57, HIP/Art Resource; p. 68, Shutterstock.com; p. 75, Lee Jae-Won/Reuters/Corbis; p. 82, Peter Morgan/Reuters/Corbis; p. 90, Bryan Bedder/Getty Images; p. 97, Historical Picture Archive/Corbis; p. 105, H. Armstrong Roberts/ClassicStock/Corbis; p. 112, The Art Archive/Museo Ciudad Mexico/Gianni Dagli Orti; p. 119, Fotolia.com; p. 126, Shutterstock.com

Library of Congress Cataloging-in-Publication Data

Broukal, Milada.
  What a world reading : amazing stories from around the globe / Milada Broukal. — 2nd ed.
    p. cm. — (What a world reading : amazing stories from around the globe series)
  Includes index.
  Previous ed.: 2004.
  ISBN 0-13-247267-8 (v. 1) — ISBN 0-13-247796-3 (v. 2) — ISBN 0-13-138201-2 (v. 3) 1. English language—Textbooks for foreign speakers. 2. Readers—Manners and customs.
  PE1128.B7165 2010
  428.6'4—dc22

                                                                                              2010020089

ISBN-13: 978-0-13-247796-3
ISBN-10: 0-13-247796-3

PEARSON LONGMAN ON THE WEB

Pearsonlongman.com offers online resources for teachers and students. Access our Companion Websites, our online catalog, and our local offices around the world.

Visit us at **www.pearsonlongman.com**.

Printed in the United States of America
5 6 7 8 9 10–V011–15 14 13

CONTENTS

INTRODUCTION

What a World: Amazing Stories from Around the Globe—the series

This series now has two strands: a reading strand and a listening strand. Both strands explore linked topics from around the world and across history. They can be used separately or together for maximum exploration of content and development of essential reading and listening skills.

	Reading Strand	**Listening Strand**
Level 1 (Beginning)	*What a World Reading 1, 2e*	*What a World Listening 1*
Level 2 (High-Beginning)	*What a World Reading 2, 2e*	*What a World Listening 2*
Level 3 (Intermediate)	*What a World Reading 3, 2e*	*What a World Listening 3*

What a World Reading 2, 2e—a high-beginning reader

It is the second in a three-book series of readings for English language learners. The 18 units in this book correspond thematically with the units in *What a World Listening 2*. Each topic is about a different person, society, place, custom, or organization. The topics span history and the globe, from the Aztecs, to Timbuktu, to early passenger flights.

New to the Second Edition

- New and updated readings: there are eight new readings
- Critical thinking questions have been added in every unit to develop students' thinking skills
- Internet Activities have been added for every unit to build students' Internet research skills; these activities are in the Appendices at the back of the book.

Unit Structure and Approach

BEFORE YOU READ opens with a picture of the person, people, place, custom, or organization featured in the unit. Prereading questions follow. Their purpose is to motivate students to read, encourage predictions about the content of the reading, and involve the students' own experiences when possible. Vocabulary can be presented as the need arises.

READING passages should first be done individually by skimming for the general content. The teacher may wish to explain the bolded vocabulary words at this point. The students should then do a second, closer reading. Further reading(s) can be done aloud.

VOCABULARY exercises focus on the boldfaced words in the reading. There are three types of vocabulary exercises. Both *Meaning* and *Words That Go Together* are definition exercises that encourage students to work out the meanings of words from the context. *Meaning* focuses on single words. *Words That Go Together* focuses on collocations or groups of words which are easier to learn together the way they are used in the language. The third exercise, *Use,* reinforces the vocabulary further by making students use the words or collocations in a meaningful, yet possibly different, context. This section can be done during or after the reading phase, or both.

COMPREHENSION exercises appear in each unit and consist of *Understanding the Reading, Remembering Details,* and *Making Inferences.* All confirm the content of the text either in general or in detail. These exercises for developing reading skills can be done individually, in pairs, in small groups, or as a class. It is preferable to do these exercises in conjunction with the text, since they are not meant to test memory. The comprehension exercises end with *Tell the Story,* which is a speaking activity.

DISCUSSION questions encourage students to bring their own ideas and imagination to the related topics in each reading. They can also provide insights into cultural similarities and differences.

CRITICAL THINKING questions give students the opportunity to develop thinking skills (comparing and contrasting cultural customs, recognizing personal attitudes and values, etc.).

WRITING exercises provide the stimulus for students to write sentences about the reading. Teachers should use their own discretion when deciding whether or not to correct the writing exercises.

SPELLING AND PUNCTUATION exercises provide basic rules and accompanying activities for spelling or punctuation, using examples from the readings.

Additional Activities

INTERNET ACTIVITIES (in the Appendices) give students the opportunity to develop their Internet research skills. Each activity can be done in a classroom setting or if the students have Internet access, as homework leading to a presentation or discussion in class. There is an Internet activity for each unit and it is always related to the theme of the unit. It helps students evaluate websites for their reliability and gets them to process and put together the information in an organized way.

SELF-TESTS after Unit 9 and Unit 18 review comprehension, vocabulary, and spelling and punctuation in a multiple-choice format.

✳ ✳ ✳ ✳ ✳

The **Answer Key** for *What a World Reading 2, 2e,* is available at the following website: http://www.pearsonlongman.com/whataworld.

WHO IS THE MOST IMPORTANT PERSON FROM HISTORY?

you read

before

Answer these questions.

1. What do you think is the most important invention in history?

2. What do you think the machine in the picture does?

3. Were books always easy to make and to get? Why or why not?

WHO IS THE MOST IMPORTANT PERSON FROM HISTORY?

1   What person from history has the greatest **effect** on our lives today? Recently, a group of many different experts decided it was a man named Johann Gutenberg. Gutenberg is famous for inventing printing, but he didn't really invent it. He invented a better way of printing.

2   For hundreds of years people used blocks of wood to print. They used a knife to cut words in the block of wood. They made the words **backward**. Then they covered the block with ink and **pressed** it onto paper. When they pulled the paper from the inky blocks, the words appeared on the paper in the right direction. In Korea and China, people printed with metal type instead of wood. Either way, printing was difficult and very slow. People usually wrote books **by hand**, so it took several years to make one copy of a book.

3   Books were very expensive and **rare**. Only rich people could buy them, and most people could not read. As more people learned to read, books became more popular. People wanted to find a quicker, better, and less-expensive way to print books. One of these people was Johann Gutenberg.

4   Gutenberg was born in Mainz, Germany, around 1400. He was an intelligent man, and he was good at working with metal. Gutenberg probably **had no idea** how people printed in China. His idea was to make a piece of metal type for each letter of the alphabet and use the letters **over and over**. He could put the type together to make words and **arrange** the words to make pages. With ink on the type, he could press paper on them to make a page. A "printing press" machine could make hundreds of copies of a single page quickly. After that page, he could rearrange the same letters to make other words and print other pages.

5   It took Gutenberg a long time to make the type for each letter of the alphabet. When he finished the type, he didn't have enough money to make the printing press. He **borrowed** money from a man named Johann Fust. They became business **partners**. After many years, Gutenberg's printing press was ready. Gutenberg printed his first book, the Bible, around 1455.

6   Johann Fust was a good businessman. He understood the importance of Gutenberg's invention. He **took** Gutenberg **to court** because Gutenberg still owed him money. Gutenberg had no money, so Fust took Gutenberg's printing press and started his own business. He printed and sold more Bibles and kept half of the money. Gutenberg was sad and nearly **broke**. He died in 1468.

7   Today people remember Johann Gutenberg. The city of Mainz has a **statue** of him and a museum. His original printing press is in the museum. They print

several pages a day to show that it is in good condition. There are only twenty-one complete copies of the original Bible. They are some of the most expensive books in the world. In 1987, part of a Gutenberg Bible sold for $5.3 million.

VOCABULARY

MEANING

Write the correct words in the blanks.

arrange	borrowed	effect	pressed	statue
backward	broke	partners	rare	

1. Gutenberg _____ money from Fust and said he would give it back.

2. There were few books before the printing press. Books were _____.

3. Gutenberg would _____ words to make pages, and then printed the pages.

4. Gutenberg's invention was very important. It has a big _____ on our lives today.

5. People cut words _____ into blocks of wood so that the printed words would be in the right direction.

6. Gutenberg and Fust worked together and became _____ in business.

7. Before Gutenberg's printing press, people _____ blocks of wood on paper to print a page.

8. Later in his life, Gutenberg had no money and was _____.

9. The people of Mainz, Germany, wanted to remember Gutenberg, so they put a _____ of him there.

WORDS THAT GO TOGETHER

Write the correct words in the blanks.

by hand	had no idea	over and over	took . . . to court

1. The Chinese also printed on paper, but Gutenberg _____ of this. He didn't know about it.

2. Gutenberg used the metal type not just one time, but _____.

3. Before the printing press, people copied books _____.

4. Fust wanted his money back from Gutenberg. He needed help from a judge. He _____ Gutenberg _____.

USE

Work with a partner to answer the questions. Use complete sentences.

1. What do you sometimes *borrow* from another student? From a neighbor?
2. What is the name of a famous *statue*? Where is it? Why is it famous?
3. What is something that is *rare*?
4. What are some things you usually *press* with your finger?
5. What is something you do *over and over* in your English class? At home?
6. What things were made *by hand* many years ago and today are made by machines?

COMPREHENSION

UNDERSTANDING THE READING

Circle the letter of the correct answer.

1. Before Gutenberg's printing press, _____.
   a. there were other kinds of printing
   b. it was easy to print books by hand
   c. Europeans printed with metal type
   d. people only wrote books by hand

2. Gutenberg _____.
   a. had the idea for a printing press
   b. knew about printing in China
   c. had the first idea for printing
   d. was good at working with paper

3. Today, people think of Gutenberg as _____.
   a. a statue in Mainz, Germany
   b. a great inventor
   c. a great seller of Bibles
   d. sad and broke

REMEMBERING DETAILS

Reread the passage and answer the questions.

1. Where was Gutenberg born?
2. What was he good at?
3. Who did he borrow money from?
4. When did Gutenberg print his first book?
5. Where is Gutenberg's printing press?
6. How much did part of a Gutenberg Bible sell for in 1987?

MAKING INFERENCES

*All of the statements below are true. Some of them are stated directly in the reading. Others can be inferred, or guessed, from the reading. Write **S** for each stated fact. Write **I** for each inference.*

_____ 1. Gutenberg was not a good businessman.

_____ 2. Gutenberg spent most of his life and money making his printing press.

_____ 3. Gutenberg had no idea that his invention would have an effect on our lives today.

_____ 4. The Bible was the most important book in Europe at that time.

_____ 5. The Bible was the first book to be printed.

TELL THE STORY

Work with a partner or together as a class. Tell the story of Johann Gutenberg. Use your own words. Your partner or other students can ask questions about the story.

DISCUSSION

Discuss the answers to these questions with your classmates.

1. Who are some other people from history who have an effect on our lives today?

2. What is an invention that you could not live without?

3. What do you think will be the next great invention?

CRITICAL THINKING

Work with a partner. Ask each other the following questions. Discuss your answers.

1. Fust would not be able to use Gutenberg's press for his own purposes today. How are inventors protected today? Why is it important to have these protections?

2. How did the invention of the printing press change the world? How did the invention of the computer change the world?

WRITING

Write six sentences or a short paragraph about an invention that is important to your life.

EXAMPLE: *The most important invention for me is the cell phone. I use it many times a day.*

_____

_____

(continued)

_____

_____

_____

_____

SPELLING AND PUNCTUATION

SILENT LETTERS: *K* AND *W*

The Silent *k*

The silent *k* usually comes at the beginning of a word and is followed by the letter *n*.
  *They used a **kn**ife to cut words in the block of wood.*

The Silent *w*

The silent *w* usually comes at the beginning of a word and is followed by the letter *r*.
  *People usually **wr**ote books by hand.*

A. *Circle the correctly spelled word in each group. You may use a dictionary.*

1.	rist	wrist	rwist	**4.**	nit	knit	nkit
2.	nee	nkee	knee	**5.**	rinkle	rwinkle	wrinkle
3.	knock	nock	nkock	**6.**	wrob	rob	rwob

B. *Complete the words with* **kn, n, wr,** *or* **r.**

1. In Gutenberg's time, people _____ote books by hand.

2. Gutenberg had no _____owledge of printing in China.

3. Fust _____ew he could make money from the _____ew invention.

4. People _____eeded books to _____ead.

5. Only the _____ich could _____ead and _____ite.

6. _____iters liked the printing press since their books could _____each more people.

7. We _____ow _____ow the importance of Gutenberg's invention.

C. *Write sentences using the words you circled in Part A.*

_____

_____

_____

_____

_____

Go to page 137 for the Internet Activity.

DID YOU KNOW?

- The world's oldest printed book is a copy of the *Diamond Sutra*—a sacred Buddhist text—which was printed in China in 868 BCE.
- Printing didn't advance quickly in China because the Chinese script has thousands of different characters.
- The technological breakthrough of the printing press has been compared to the invention of the Internet.
- A copy of James Audubon's *Birds of America* sold for $8.8 million in 2000 making it the most expensive printed book.

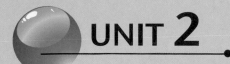

WHAT ARE FATTENING ROOMS?

before you read

Answer these questions.

1. Do women in Europe and North America prefer to be thin or fat?

2. Do you think a thin person is healthier than a fat person?

3. Is it easier for you to gain weight (become fatter) or to lose weight (become slimmer)?

WHAT ARE FATTENING ROOMS?

1   In North America and Europe, most women want to be **slim**. There, a slim woman is a beautiful woman. There, a slim woman is healthy and careful about what she eats. But in some parts of the world, women want to be fat. In many parts of Africa, a fat woman is a beautiful woman. How fat? There is no **limit**. If a woman is fat, she is healthy and rich. If a woman is slim, that means she is a worker with little money and not enough food to eat. Also, people believe that a slim woman will be sick or that she can't have children. A fat woman has enough food to eat, so she is healthy and will have many healthy babies.

2   To help girls and women look healthy and beautiful, people in central Africa send them to a fattening room. The tradition of fattening rooms is an old one and an important part of a girl's life. After a girl goes to a fattening room, her family and her village say that she is a woman. The fattening room is usually in or near the family's house. In the fattening room, a girl sits on a special chair until it is time to eat. Then she sits on the floor on a **mat** made of leaves. She also sleeps on the floor. Her mother gives her bowls of food, such as rice, yams, and beans—the **kinds of** foods that help her get fat. She also drinks a lot of water.

3   In the fattening room, the girl does not move very much. She can only eat, sleep, and get fatter. Her only visitors are women who teach her how to sit, walk, and talk in front of her **future** husband. They also give her advice about cleaning, sewing, and cooking. It is boring to be in the fattening room for so long with nothing to do, but the girl **doesn't mind**. She knows that it is important for her.

4   In southeastern Nigeria, brides go to a fattening room or a fattening farm before they get married. They cannot leave the farm for many weeks. At the end of this time, but before the wedding, the brides walk through the village so everyone can **admire** their big bodies. After a woman is married, she can also go to a fattening room. She may go several times because it is important for her to stay fat. A man wants his wife to be fat so other people will think that he is a rich and **responsible** man.

5   If parents don't send their daughters to a fattening room, their friends and relatives may laugh at them. They will say that the parents are not **doing their duty. In the old days**, girls sometimes stayed in a fattening room for two years. Today, some families cannot **afford** more than a few months. Also, fattening rooms are not very popular in cities now. In cities, health education and Western culture have a big effect on people's ideas. But in villages, this traditional custom continues.

6   In Niger, they have a festival to celebrate the heaviest woman. Here, women have a **contest** to see who is the fattest. On the morning of the contest, the women eat **enormous** amounts of food and drink lots of water. The fattest woman is the winner. She gets a prize—more food!

VOCABULARY

MEANING

Write the correct words in the blanks.

admire	contest	future	mat	slim
afford	enormous	limit	responsible	

1. In North America and Europe, women don't want to be fat; they want to be

   _____.

2. In some parts of Africa, women like to be fat. There is no _____ to how

   fat a woman can be.

3. In a fattening room, a girl sits on a _____ on the floor when she eats.

4. Women teach her how to act in front of the man she is going to marry. She learns

   how to act for her _____ husband.

5. People in the village like the big bodies of the women very much. They

   _____ the women.

6. When a woman is fat, people think that her husband is a _____ man

   because he takes care of her.

7. Some families cannot _____ to keep a girl in a fattening room for a

   long time because it is expensive.

8. In Niger, many women want to be the fattest woman, so they have a _____.

9. Women eat _____ amounts of food to get fat.

WORDS THAT GO TOGETHER

Write the correct words in the blanks.

doesn't mind	doing their duty	in the old days	kinds of

1. The girl is bored in the fattening room, but she _____. She

   knows the fattening room is important for her life.

2. In the fattening room, girls eat the _____ foods that help

   make them fat.

3. _____, girls stayed in a fattening room for a long time, but

   today they only stay for a few months.

4. If parents don't send their daughters to fattening rooms, people will say they are not

   helping their daughters. People think the parents are not _____.

USE

Work with a partner to answer the questions. Use complete sentences.

1. Where would you like to go on a *future* vacation?
2. What quality do you *admire* in a man or woman?
3. What can't you *afford* to buy this year?
4. What are some kinds of *contests* in your country?
5. What must you do to be *slim*?
6. What *kinds of* exercise do you enjoy most?

COMPREHENSION

UNDERSTANDING THE READING

Circle the letter of the correct answer.

1. In some parts of Africa, people think a slim girl _____.
   - **a.** is healthy
   - **b.** will have many babies
   - **c.** is not healthy
   - **d.** is beautiful

2. A girl goes to a fattening room _____.
   - **a.** only to learn to sew and cook
   - **b.** to become a woman
   - **c.** for one week only
   - **d.** to be alone and think

3. Today, fattening rooms _____.
   - **a.** are still popular in villages
   - **b.** are not popular anymore
   - **c.** are popular in villages and big cities
   - **d.** are only popular with very rich families

REMEMBERING DETAILS

Reread the passage and fill in the blanks.

1. In some parts of Africa, people believe that a slim girl will be

   _____.

2. In the fattening room, the girl sleeps on the _____.

3. Women visitors give her advice about _____,

   _____, and _____.

4. When a man has a fat wife, people think he is a rich and _____

   man.

(continued)

5. Today, fattening rooms are not popular in _____.

6. In a contest in Niger, the heaviest woman is the _____.

MAKING INFERENCES

*All of the statements below are true. Some of them are stated directly in the reading. Others can be inferred, or guessed, from the reading. Write **S** for each stated fact. Write **I** for each inference.*

_____ 1. In villages, girls still go to fattening rooms.

_____ 2. A woman with an education will probably not go to a fattening room.

_____ 3. A woman may go to a fattening room several times in her life.

_____ 4. In some countries, a fat body means that the person is rich.

_____ 5. Rich men usually marry women from rich families.

TELL THE STORY

Work with a partner or together as a class. Tell the story of fattening rooms. Use your own words. Your partner or other students can ask questions about the story.

DISCUSSION

Discuss the answers to these questions with your classmates.

1. What kinds of things do people do to change their bodies? Which of these can be bad for their health?

2. What makes a man or a woman attractive in your country? What makes a man or woman attractive to you?

3. A person's size is not important, but in some societies people still think it is important. How can we change our society to accept people of different sizes?

CRITICAL THINKING

Work with a partner. Ask each other the following questions. Discuss your answers.

1. Some traditional customs are good for people, but others can be harmful. Do you think the custom of fattening rooms is good or bad for African women? Why? In your country, what traditional customs should not change because they are good for people? What customs should change? Why?

2. People with more education are generally healthier, wealthier, and live longer than people with little education. Why do you think this is so? Why does education have such a big effect on peoples' lives and health?

WRITING

Write six sentences or a short paragraph about how you try to stay healthy and look good.

EXAMPLE: *I don't eat many cakes and cookies because I don't want to gain weight.*

I try to eat fruits and vegetables. I don't go to a gym, but I walk a lot.

_____

_____

_____

_____

_____

_____

SPELLING AND PUNCTUATION

SUFFIXES: DOUBLING CONSONANTS IN ONE-SYLLABLE WORDS

A *suffix* is a letter or group of letters that we add to the end of a word to change its meaning or its form. We usually double the consonant in a one-syllable word with a short vowel sound before adding a suffix beginning with a vowel. Some of these suffixes are *-y*, *-ing*, *-er*, *-est*, and *-ed*.

fat + *-er* = **fatter**	*fat* + *-est* = **fattest**
slim + *-er* = **slimmer**	*slim* + *-est* = **slimmest**
win + *-er* = **winner**	*win* + *-ing* – **winning**

A. *Underline the misspelled words. Write the correct words on the lines. Some sentences have more than one incorrect word.*

1. You can see some of the bigest women in Niger.   _____

2. On her wedding day, it was hot and suny.   _____

3. Her parents are planing to put her in a
   fatening room this year.   _____

4. She is geting ready to be a bride.   _____

5. She is siting on a special chair in the
   fatening room.   _____

6. Eating a lot of food will make her the winer.   _____

7. In the United States, women spend a lot
   of time on sliming exercises.   _____

8. What are we eating for diner?   _____

(continued)

9. She stoped walking and runing to put on weight. _____

10. She was hopping to win the contest. _____

B. *Write two sentences with words you corrected in Part A.*

_____

_____

 *Go to page 137 for the Internet Activity.*

| **DID YOU KNOW?** | • In many Pacific Island countries, large size is considered a mark of beauty and social status.
• Arab women and young girls in Mauritania (West Africa) go to fattening farms, too.
• In the Wodaabe tribe of the Niger, Africa, it is the men who put on makeup and dance in a beauty contest judged by women. | |

WHERE CAN YOU FIND A LIVING GODDESS?

WHERE CAN YOU FIND A LIVING GODDESS?

1   You can find a living goddess in Nepal. In fact, there is more than one of them! Some cities in Nepal actually have several goddesses. However, the best-known goddess lives in the city of Katmandu. She is called the Royal Kumari, or *Kumari Devi*. This young woman lives in a palace in the center of the city. In some South Asian countries, such as Nepal and India, the tradition of worshipping a Kumari Devi is a popular and ancient one that continues today.

2   A Kumari Devi is a girl, chosen when she is very young (usually between the ages of four and seven) to be worshipped by both Hindus and Buddhists. The **selection** of a goddess is quite **complicated**. Five priests and an astrologer must take many things into consideration when choosing a new Kumari. The girl must be from the Sakya community and have the right **horoscope**. She must be in excellent health; she must never have had any diseases or any **blemishes**. The girl must next pass the test of the thirty-two perfections of a goddess. She must "have eyelashes like a cow and a voice soft and clear as a duck's." In addition, her hair and eyes must be very black, her hands and feet must be delicate, and she must have a set of twenty teeth. She must also pass tests to show that she is fearless and is always **serene**. For the final test, she must pick out the **personal belongings** of the **previous** Kumari from the belongings that are put in front of her. If she does this, then there is **no doubt** that she is the Kumari.

3   After she is chosen, she walks from the temple to her palace. She walks on a white cloth, and this is the last time she will walk outside the palace. From now on, she will only leave the palace on ceremonial occasions. At these times, she will be carried by attendants on her gold chair. She will never wear shoes, and her feet are now sacred. She will always wear red, her hair will be in a topknot,[1] and on her forehead will be painted the "fire eye" as a symbol of her special powers of perception. People believe that if they see her for even a second, it will bring good luck. Crowds often wait below her window at the palace to try to get a look at her. **Government officials** and people who have connections are able to see her at the palace where she sits on a throne. She receives them in silence and offers them her feet to touch and kiss to get her blessing. Even the president of Nepal goes to get the Kumari's blessing.

4   The Kumari stops being a goddess as soon as she reaches **puberty**. Also, she stops being a goddess if she has a serious illness or an injury and returns to her family. Then selection starts for a new Kumari. The old Kumari receives a **pension** from the government which is about twice the **minimum wage** or about four times the average income in this poor country. There is a superstition that it is bad luck to marry a Kumari. However, most Kumaris get married and have children just like everyone else.

---

[1] *topknot:* hair that is tied together on the top of your head

VOCABULARY

MEANING

Write the correct words in the blanks.

| blemishes | horoscope | previous | selection |
| complicated | pension | puberty | serene |

1. The _____, or choice, of the right goddess follows tradition.

2. It is difficult, or _____, to find the right girl.

3. The priests look at the young girl's _____, or the position of the stars and planets, when she was born.

4. The young girl must have no marks on her skin, or _____ on her body.

5. The young girl must always look calm and peaceful, or _____.

6. The _____ Kumari, or the Kumari before the new one, leaves her old clothes behind.

7. The young girl stops being a goddess when she can have a baby, or at _____.

8. The old Kumari gets a regular payment from the government called a " _____."

WORDS THAT GO TOGETHER

Write the correct words in the blanks.

| government officials | minimum wage | no doubt | personal belongings |

1. The young girl must pick out the things such as clothes or _____ of the old Kumari.

2. After this last test, there is no question, or _____, she is the real Kumari.

3. People in government positions, or _____, go to touch her feet.

4. The old Kumari receives twice what employers give to workers, or the _____.

USE

Work with a partner to answer the questions. Use complete sentences.

1. What is your sign on the *horoscope*?
2. Where do you keep your *personal belongings* in the classroom?
3. What is *complicated* to learn in English grammar?
4. What is the *minimum wage* in your country right now?
5. Where can you see *government officials* in your country?
6. At what age do people usually *get a pension* from the government?

COMPREHENSION

UNDERSTANDING THE READING

Circle the letter of the correct answer.

1. To become a goddess, a girl must _____.
   a. come from a family of priests and astrologers
   b. be related to the previous goddess
   c. write poetry and see into the future
   d. meet a large number of requirements

2. The life of a Kumari is _____.
   a. protected and ceremonial
   b. exciting and varied
   c. like that of most Nepalese children
   d. like that of most adults

3. The role of a living goddess _____.
   a. is for a lifetime
   b. brings a girl great riches
   c. ends when the girl marries
   d. often lasts less than ten years

REMEMBERING DETAILS

Reread the passage and answer the questions.

1. Who worships the goddesses in Nepal?
2. What kinds of eyes, hair, hands, and feet must a goddess have?
3. What is the final test a girl must pass before becoming a Kumari?
4. When is the goddess allowed to leave the palace?
5. Why is the "fire eye" painted on the Kumari's forehead?
6. Why do people try to see the Kumari?

MAKING INFERENCES

All of the statements below are true. Some of them are stated directly in the reading. Others can be inferred, or guessed, from the reading. Write S for each stated fact. Write I for each inference.

_____ 1. Worshipping the Kumari is based on an old tradition.

_____ 2. Only a very special child could pass all the tests to be a goddess.

_____ 3. A Kumari has responsibilities as well as privileges.

_____ 4. A Kumari is not free to do as she likes.

_____ 5. A Kumari can eventually get married and have children.

TELL THE STORY

Work with a partner or together as a class. Tell the story of the living goddess. Use your own words. Your partner or other students can ask questions about the story.

DISCUSSION

Discuss the answers to these questions with your classmates.

1. What people in your culture are believed to have special powers or abilities? Do you believe in them as well? Why or why not?

2. Do you think that a child who is chosen to be Kumari Devi is fortunate? What do you think are the advantages and disadvantages of being chosen?

3. What qualities do you think a goddess should have? What would be on your list of thirty-two perfections for physical, intellectual, and character traits?

CRITICAL THINKING

Work with a partner. Ask each other the following questions. Discuss your answers.

1. What purpose do you think the goddess tradition has in Nepalese culture? Why do think the Nepalese keep this tradition alive today? What ancient tradition does your culture still observe? Do you think it's a good thing to keep that tradition alive? Why or why not?

2. What does it mean to have "special powers of perception"? Do you believe there are people with strong powers of perception? Do you believe in psychics and fortune-tellers? Why or why not? Do you think there are people with certain powers that others don't have? Who are they?

WRITING

Write six sentences or a short paragraph about a tradition in your country.

EXAMPLE: *In my country, it is a tradition to buy new clothes for New Year's Day.*
We eat a special, big dinner.

_____

_____

_____

_____

_____

_____

SPELLING AND PUNCTUATION

EI OR *IE*?

Here is the general rule for using *ei* or *ie*:
*Use **i** before **e***
*Except after **c**,*
*Or when sounded like **a***
*As in n**ei**ghbor or w**ei**gh.*

- We use *i* before *e*.
  The **priests** select the goddess.

- We use *ei* after *c*.
  The goddess **receives** people in her palace.

- We use *ei* when it sounds like *a*.
  The present Kumari is **eight** years old.

- There are exceptions to the rule! Here are some exceptions.
  ancient   foreign   science   neither   their   leisure

A. *Circle the correctly spelled words.*

1. Worshipping a goddess is an (ancient / anceint) tradition.

2. The girl must always be serene even when she sees (weird / wierd) things.

3. In a test, she must choose the right objects from (peices / pieces) of clothing and other belongings placed in front of her.

4. Her (reign / riegn) as goddess ends at puberty.

5. It is a great honor (bieng / being) chosen to be a Kumari.

6. She cannot go out with her (friends / freinds) anymore.

7. She can (niether / neither) leave the palace nor do what she likes.

8. People (beleive / believe) the Kumari has a strong power.

9. They think (their / thier) luck will get better if they see the Kumari.

10. Her pension is (sufficeint / sufficient) for her to live a comfortable life.

B. *Write three sentences with* **ei** *or* **ie** *words.*

_____

_____

_____

Go to page 138 for the Internet Activity.

DID YOU KNOW ?

- Nepal is among the poorest and least-developed countries in the world, with 40 percent of its population living below the poverty line.
- In India, a Kumari is usually chosen for one day and is worshipped accordingly on certain festivals.
- Every September the Kumari Devi is taken out on her chair into the square for the Kumari festival attended by thousands of people who want to see her and get her blessings.
- The Kumari appears for tourists through a carved window at her residence in the square.

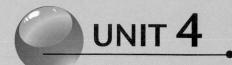
UNIT 4

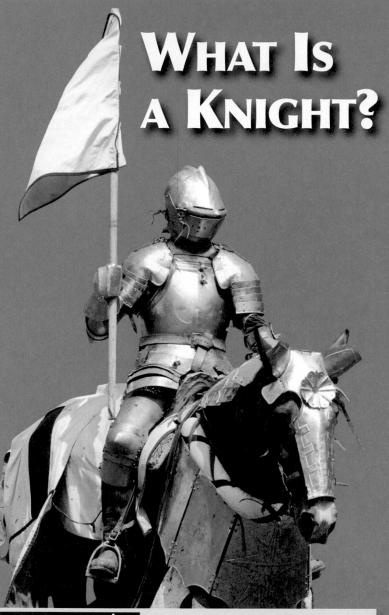

WHAT IS A KNIGHT?

you read

before

Answer these questions.

1. Who are some famous knights from books and movies?

2. What were knights like?

3. Are there still knights today?

WHAT IS A KNIGHT?

1   The role of the knight changed over the centuries. In the beginning, a knight was just a soldier. As time passed, a knight was a powerful soldier and a nobleman. A typical knight was a man who lived between the ninth and sixteenth centuries in Europe. He promised to fight for the king for forty days of each year, and **in return** he received land from the king and a position in the king's court. He could also take anything of value from battles he fought.

2   Not everyone **had the right** to be a knight. A knight's firstborn son had the right to become a knight as well as to **inherit** his father's land. If a man was from royalty or was the son of someone with a **title**, he had the **opportunity** to become a knight. A man could also become a knight if he was very brave in battle.

3   It took about fourteen years to train to be a knight. At about age seven, the son of a noble became a *page.* This was like a junior assistant to a knight. His new master was a relative or a family friend. The page lived in his master's home. He learned to hunt, use a bow and arrow, and take care of his master's **weapons** and armor. Between the ages of fourteen and sixteen, a page became a *squire.* He now had more **responsibilities**. He looked after his master's horse and helped him dress and undress. He helped him put on his armor for battle. This took many hours because the armor weighed 50 pounds! He learned how to fight with a sword and how to fight on a horse. If he was successful, he became a knight when he was about twenty-one.

4   Not every squire would become a knight. He had to pass tests of strength and skill with weapons. He also had to prove he had enough income. Being a knight was expensive: he had to have three horses—one for baggage, one for riding, and a heavy horse for fighting. He also needed several attendants as well as armor, which was expensive. If the squire didn't have money, he would be a squire to other knights for the rest of his life. If he was successful, he became a knight in a special ceremony. On that day, he **kneeled** in front a knight who **tapped** his shoulder with a sword. Then he became a knight and was addressed as "Sir."

5   Knights had to behave according to a set of rules. This was known as the "code of chivalry." The knight had to promise to obey his lord and show courage, honesty, loyalty, and strength. He had to protect the poor and weak, especially women. He had to fight for justice and fairness for everyone. Knights also followed the rules of "courtly love": they had to **fall in love with** a woman of equal or higher **rank**. A knight had to worship his love from a distance and could not tell her he loved her.

6   With new inventions, such as gunpowder and firearms, it was no longer useful for knights to wear armor. Today, knights have become a legend, although the Queen of England still gives a knighthood to people who have **contributed to** society. They kneel in front of the Queen and rise with the title of honor, "Sir."

MEANING

Write the correct words in the blanks.

inherit	opportunity	responsibilities	title
kneeled	rank	tapped	weapons

1. When a knight died, his son could take over, or _____, his land.

2. A person with a _____ such as *Prince* or *Duke* before his name could become a knight.

3. If you were royalty, you had the possibility, or _____, to become a knight.

4. A knight had _____ such as a sword to fight with.

5. A squire had _____, or duties, such as putting on his master's armor.

6. In a special ceremony, a squire _____, or had to get down on his knees, in front of a knight.

7. A knight could love a woman of the same or higher position, or _____, as himself.

8. The knight _____, or gently struck, the squire's shoulder with a sword to make him a knight.

WORDS THAT GO TOGETHER

Write the correct words in the blanks.

contributed to	fall in love with	had the right	in return

1. A knight fought for the king, and as payment back, or _____, the king gave him land.

2. The son of a knight _____, or the permission by law, to become a knight one day.

3. Knights would often have deep feelings for, or _____, ladies of the court.

4. Queen Elizabeth II of England gives a knighthood to people who have helped, or _____, society in some way.

USE

Work with a partner to answer the questions. Use complete sentences.

1. What is your *title* in your language?
2. Who will you *inherit* something from?
3. What are two of your *responsibilities* at home?
4. At what age did you first *fall in love with* someone?
5. What would be a good *opportunity* to practice your English?
6. When do you *have the right to* vote in your society?

COMPREHENSION

UNDERSTANDING THE READING

Circle the letter of the correct answer.

1. To have the opportunity to become a knight, a young man had to _____.
   a. be the son of a noble
   b. own a lot of property
   c. have a position in the king's court
   d. be the youngest son of a knight

2. During his training, a young man _____.
   a. fought for his master
   b. lived in the king's castle
   c. learned skills from his master
   d. worked with other knights for twenty-one years

3. The code of chivalry was a _____.
   a. set of rules for fighting
   b. guide for values and behavior
   c. secret language among the knights
   d. group of laws that everyone had to live by

REMEMBERING DETAILS

Reread the passage and answer the questions.

1. What did the knight receive in return for fighting for the king?
2. What did the page learn from his master?
3. What tests did the young man have to pass to become a knight?
4. What happened if a squire didn't have money?
5. Whom did the knight promise to protect?
6. When were knights with armor no longer necessary?

MAKING INFERENCES

*All of the statements below are true. Some of them are stated directly in the reading. Others can be inferred, or guessed, from the reading. Write **S** for each stated fact. Write **I** for each inference.*

_____ 1. The knight was a powerful soldier who fought for the king.

_____ 2. It took many years of training to become a knight.

_____ 3. There was little chance that even a brave man from a poor village would become a knight.

_____ 4. It took a young man of great character and strength to become a knight.

_____ 5. Physical strength is no longer a requirement for knighthood.

TELL THE STORY

Work with a partner or together as a class. Tell the story of what a knight was. Use your own words. Your partner or other students can ask questions about the story.

DISCUSSION

Discuss the answers to these questions with your classmates.

1. Do you think knights really lived by the "code of chivalry"? Why did knights become the subjects of legends? What interests you the most about the knights?

2. Who are fighters from legend in your culture? When did they live? How did they train? What code did they live by? What did they fight for? What made them famous?

3. What do you think the life of a knight was like? What were the advantages of being a knight? What were the disadvantages? How do you think a knight showed his love for a woman from a distance?

CRITICAL THINKING

Work with a partner. Ask each other the following questions. Discuss your answers.

1. What does the term *chivalrous* mean? What are some examples of chivalrous behavior? Do you think chivalry exists today? Does chivalry have any place in modern society? Why or why not?

2. What countries in the world still have royalty? What purposes do they serve? What privileges do they have? Is there a place for royalty in the modern world? Why or why not? Who takes the place of royalty today?

WRITING

Write six sentences or a short paragraph about royalty.

EXAMPLE: *The British have a queen.*

She lives in Buckingham Palace.

There was a movie about her.

_____

_____

_____

_____

_____

_____

SPELLING AND PUNCTUATION

WORDS WITH THE SAME SOUNDS

Some words have the same sounds, but they have different meanings and spellings. These words are called *homophones*.

knight	*We read about the adventures of the **knight** in armor.*
night	*I read the story at **night**.*
sun	*His armor shone in the **sun**.*
son	*His **son** could be a knight.*
their	*We read about **their** adventures.*
they're	***They're** legends today.*
there	***There** is a special ceremony today.*

Circle the correct word for each sentence.

1. It took (ours / hours) to put on armor.

2. He wore armor (for / four) protection.

3. The knight's (role / roll) changed over time.

4. Not everyone had the (write / right) to be a knight.

5. How much does armor (way / weigh)?

6. It took a long time (to / two) train to be knight.

7. He rode a (hoarse / horse) when he fought.

8. Knights protected the (week / weak).

9. (It's / Its) called a *knighthood*.

10. (Their / There) names have the title "Sir."

Go to page 138 for the Internet Activity.

DID YOU KNOW?

- The modern military salute comes from the days when knights in armor raised their visors to identify themselves when they rode past the king.
- Women that are knighted by the Queen take the title "Dame"—Dame Elizabeth Taylor, Dame Julie Andrews.
- If a knight was captured alive in battle, he could be offered back to his family for a ransom.
- Early knights wore a type of armor called chainmail. It looked like knitting except it was made of metal. Under this they wore a padded jacket.

WHO REACHED THE SOUTH POLE FIRST?

before you read

Answer these questions.

1. What is the coldest place you ever visited?

2. What qualities must you have to be an explorer?

3. What would you like to explore (for example, the Andes, a cave, etc.)?

WHO REACHED THE SOUTH POLE FIRST?

1   In 1900, two places in the world never seen by humans were lands of snow and ice—the North Pole and the South Pole.

2   As a young man in Norway, Roald Amundsen read about explorers who tried to reach the North Pole, and he wanted to reach it. It became his dream. The first step was to learn how to sail, so Amundsen went to sea as a worker on a ship when he was twenty-two. Later, he worked on a ship that went to Antarctica. Antarctica is the coldest place on Earth. The South Pole is in the center of Antarctica. It was an exciting trip, but he did not try to reach the South Pole.

3   Amundsen sailed on many ships and **worked his way up** to the top jobs. In 1903, he was the captain of a ship **on its way** to the Arctic. This ship was the first to sail the Northwest Passage. The Northwest Passage was important because it helped people to travel from Europe to Asia.

4   Amundsen was now a famous explorer, and he started to plan his **voyage** to the North Pole. But an American named Robert Peary reached the pole before Amundsen was able to make his voyage. Amundsen wanted to be first, so he changed his plans and went to the South Pole **instead**. He heard that an English explorer named Robert Scott was on his way to the South Pole, so Amundsen sent him a message. He said that this was now a **race**.

5   When Amundsen reached Antarctica, he and four of his men started toward the South Pole. There was only ice and snow, and the wind was freezing. He had teams of dogs to pull sleds with food and tents. They climbed mountains of snow and fell through holes in the ice. Finally, they were near the South Pole. They didn't know **whether** Scott was **already** there before them. They reached the South Pole on December 14, 1911, and there was **no sign of** Scott. Amundsen won the race.

6   Scott and his group were on their way, but they were not prepared for the **extreme** weather. They did not have the right clothes, and Scott had horses instead of dogs. The horses were not **used to** the freezing weather of Antarctica, and the men had to shoot them. The men then had to carry everything. Scott and his men finally arrived at the South Pole, but thirty-three days after Amundsen's group. Scott saw the Norwegian flag and was very sad. He and his men returned to their camp. On the way, one man died. At the camp the four men didn't have **fuel** for heat.

7   People around the world were very happy for Amundsen, but they wanted to know whether Scott and his men also reached the South Pole. They waited months, but there was no news. That summer, another group of people went to look for them. They finally found the camp and the bodies of Scott and his men in their tent. They were all frozen.

8   Amundsen reached the South Pole, but he still had the **goal** to go to the North Pole. In 1926, he and his friend Umberto Nobile flew in an airship over the North Pole—another first! A few years later, Nobile's airship crashed on another Arctic trip. Amundsen went to search for him. On the way, his airplane crashed, and the great explorer died. Other people found Nobile later—he **survived**.

VOCABULARY

MEANING

Write the correct words in the blanks.

already	fuel	instead	survived	whether
extreme	goal	race	voyage	

1. Amundsen wanted to travel to the North Pole. He went on a _____.

2. Amundsen heard that another person was at the North Pole first. The person was _____ there.

3. Amundsen and Scott had a _____ to see who would reach the South Pole first.

4. Amundsen didn't know _____ Scott was already at the South Pole.

5. The weather at the South Pole was very, very cold. It was too _____ for horses.

6. Scott and his men froze to death because they had no _____ for heat.

7. After the South Pole, Amundsen decided to reach his original _____, the North Pole.

8. Amundsen died, but his friend Nobile didn't die. He _____.

9. Amundsen wanted to go to the North Pole, but he changed his plans and went to the South Pole _____.

WORDS THAT GO TOGETHER

Write the correct words in the blanks.

no sign of	on its way	used to	worked his way up

1. Amundsen got to the South Pole and didn't see Scott. There was
   _____ Scott.

2. Horses like nice weather. They are not _____ the cold
   weather of Antarctica.

3. Amundsen went to sea as a worker first. Then he _____ to be
   a captain.

4. Amundsen's ship was _____ to the Arctic when they found
   the Northwest Passage.

USE

Work with a partner to answer the questions. Use complete sentences.

1. What places in the world have *extreme* weather?
2. What kinds of *races* do you have in your country?
3. What kind of *fuel* do you use for heat? For a car? For lights?
4. What have you *already* done today?
5. What is one *goal* that you hope to reach in your life?
6. What kind of weather are you *used to*?

COMPREHENSION

UNDERSTANDING THE READING

Circle the letter of the correct answer.

1. Amundsen _____.
   a. always wanted to reach the South Pole
   b. was already famous before he reached the South Pole
   c. never wanted to go to the North Pole
   d. never wanted to be the captain of a ship

2. Amundsen _____.

    a. reached the South Pole after Scott

    b. reached the South Pole before Peary

    c. reached the South Pole before Scott

    d. reached the South Pole after Peary

3. Amundsen _____.

    a. found Nobile's airship after the crash

    b. died as he looked for his friend Nobile

    c. died with Nobile in the airship crash

    d. died after he found Nobile and the crashed airship

REMEMBERING DETAILS

Reread the passage and answer the questions.

1. Where did Amundsen's ship go in 1903?
2. What country did Robert Peary, the North Pole explorer, come from?
3. When did Amundsen reach the South Pole?
4. When did Scott reach the South Pole?
5. Where did they find the bodies of Scott and his men?
6. What did Amundsen and Nobile do together?

MAKING INFERENCES

*All of the statements below are true. Some of them are stated directly in the reading. Others can be inferred, or guessed, from the reading. Write **S** for each stated fact. Write **I** for each inference.*

_____ **1.** Scott was not an experienced explorer like Amundsen.

_____ **2.** Scott used horses to pull his sleds.

_____ **3.** Scott and his men froze because they had no fuel for heat.

_____ **4.** Future explorers learned a lot from Scott's death.

_____ **5.** Amundsen was the first person to reach the South Pole and the first to fly over the North Pole.

TELL THE STORY

Work with a partner or together as a class. Tell the story of who reached the South Pole first. Use your own words. Your partner or other students can ask questions about the story.

DISCUSSION

Discuss the answers to these questions with your classmates.

1. Some people like to prepare to go on a trip, and some people do not. What preparations do you make before you go on a trip? Do you like preparing for a trip? Why or why not?

2. Why do people go on difficult and dangerous voyages? Would you like to go on a difficult or dangerous voyage? Why or why not?

3. Which would you prefer to visit: the North Pole, a tropical rainforest, or the Sahara Desert? Talk about your choice.

CRITICAL THINKING

Work with a partner. Ask each other the following questions. Discuss your answers.

1. Many explorers have died during their voyages of discovery. What contributions did they make to the world? Were their voyages worth their lives?

2. Who are some modern-day adventurers and explorers? What type of person is willing to endure hardship and risk his or her life to explore a new place and have adventure? Are there any places left to explore in the modern world?

WRITING

Write six sentences or a short paragraph about the place you chose for Discussion question 3.

EXAMPLE: *I would like to visit the Sahara Desert. I saw it in films, and it looks very beautiful.*

_____

_____

_____

_____

_____

_____

SPELLING AND PUNCTUATION

COMMAS BEFORE *AND, BUT,* AND *OR*

We use a comma before the words *and, but,* and *or* when they join two sentences together.

> *Amundsen was now a famous explorer. He started to plan his voyage to the North Pole.* (two sentences)

> *Amundsen was now a famous explorer,* **and** *he started to plan his voyage to the North Pole.* (and joins two sentences)

> *Scott and his men were on their way. They were not prepared for the extreme weather.* (two sentences)

> *Scott and his men were on their way,* **but** *they were not prepared for the extreme weather.* (but joins two sentences)

We do <u>not</u> use a comma before *and, but,* and *or* in a simple sentence. In a simple sentence, *and, but,* and *or* join two nouns, two adjectives, two adverbs, or two verbs.

NOUN   NOUN

> *He had teams of dogs to pull sleds with <u>food</u> and <u>tents</u>.*

       VERB   VERB

> *They didn't <u>eat</u> or <u>sleep</u> for days.*

Put commas in the correct places. Some sentences do not need commas.

1. Amundsen read about explorers going to the polar regions and he wanted to go there, too.
2. First, he worked on a boat that went to Antarctica but didn't go to the South Pole.
3. Amundsen gathered supplies and men.
4. They were tired but happy when they reached the South Pole.
5. There was snow and ice everywhere but the men weren't worried.
6. It was important for Amundsen to be the first to get to the North Pole or the South Pole.
7. Amundsen had dogs to pull the sleds but Scott had horses.
8. People had no news of Scott or his men.

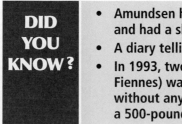 *Go to page 139 for the Internet Activity.*

DID YOU KNOW?

- Amundsen had planned everything carefully in advance and had a shorter route to the Pole.
- A diary telling their story was found in Scott's tent.
- In 1993, two Englishmen (Dr. Mike Stroud and Ranulph Fiennes) walked across the continent of Antarctica without any support from other people, each man pulling a 500-pound sledge.

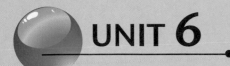

WHAT IS THE ROYAL FLYING DOCTOR SERVICE?

before you read

Answer these questions.

1. If you are far from a city or town in your country, how do you get medical help?

2. Is it difficult to get medical help in an emergency? Why or why not?

3. What are some methods of communication and transportation that make it possible to get medical help quickly?

WHAT IS THE ROYAL FLYING DOCTOR SERVICE?

1   Most people in Australia live in cities along the coast. Very few people live in the huge middle area, where houses are far away from each other. Australians call this part of the country "the Outback." In the past, when people in the Outback **had an accident** or got very sick, there were no doctors nearby to take care of them. Today, people in the Outback can call a special **service** called the Royal Flying Doctor Service and get medical advice in a few minutes. The Royal Flying Doctors use airplanes to reach people in places that don't have doctors.

2   A **minister**, Reverend John Flynn, started the Royal Flying Doctor Service in the 1920s. He often traveled by **truck** through central and northern Australia for his church. Many times, he saw people die because there was no doctor near. He thought, "There must be some way to help these people. First, I will build **hospitals** for them."

3   Flynn worked very hard, and by 1927, there were ten small hospitals in central and northern Australia. Nurses took care of the sick and **injured** people. But Flynn was not **satisfied**. He had hospitals and nurses, but he needed doctors. And there was another problem. If he had doctors, how could they treat people who still lived far away from the hospitals? Then, he had an idea! "The doctors can travel by airplane. We will also build a place for a plane to land near every Outback home." Many people laughed at the idea. Airplane travel in 1927 was a new and dangerous thing.

4   There was one more problem: people so far away couldn't **get in touch with** a doctor. Flynn said, "We will use a radio to send and **receive** messages." At that time, radios could not work in most of the Outback because there was no electricity. But an engineer invented a radio that worked with a foot pedal. With this invention people were able to call for help from far away.

5   Everything was ready. The Royal Flying Doctor Service began in May 1928. The Service was a great success, and Flynn was very happy. In the first year, doctors made fifty flights. They flew 18,000 miles, helped 225 people, and saved 4 lives. Flynn now wanted the Service to be in all parts of the Outback. His church did not have enough money for this plan, so the different states in Australia agreed to help. Each state built one or two hospitals.

6   In 1942, the Royal Flying Doctor Service **came up with** another good idea. Every home in the Outback got a carefully prepared **first-aid kit**. Each kit had the same drugs, bandages, and other first-aid materials. Everything in the kit had its own special number. Later, the kits had a picture of the human body with a number for each different part. When people got sick or injured, they used the radio to call the medical center. The doctor asked about the problem by number. Then the doctor told the caller to use medicine from the kit by numbers, too. For example, the

(continued)

doctor said, "Take one **pill** from number 8 every three hours," or "Put number 22 on your injured leg."

7   Today there are 3,000 medical kits, 22 hospitals, and 53 Royal Flying Doctor Service airplanes. Each year, the service helps about 274,000 people.

VOCABULARY

MEANING

Write the correct words in the blanks.

hospitals	minister	receive	service
injured	pill	satisfied	truck

1. The Royal Flying Doctors is a special medical organization. It is a _____ that helps sick people in the Outback of Australia.

2. Reverend Flynn was a _____ in his church.

3. Flynn drove a _____ around the Outback and saw many sick people die.

4. He wanted to build _____ to help the sick.

5. Flynn had nurses to help him, but he was not _____. He needed doctors, too.

6. People went to the hospital for different reasons. Some were _____, and some were sick.

7. Flynn needed a radio to send and _____ messages.

8. The instructions were to take a _____.

WORDS THAT GO TOGETHER

Write the correct words in the blanks.

came up with	first-aid kit	get in touch with	had an accident

1. In the past, when a person in the Outback _____, there wasn't a doctor to call.

2. Flynn heard about an engineer and decided to _____ him. Flynn talked to him about making a special radio.

3. Flynn always _____ new ideas to improve the Service.

4. It is important to have a _____ at home to help when someone gets sick or injured.

USE

Work with a partner to answer the questions. Use complete sentences.

1. Why is it good to have a *first-aid kit*?
2. What is a *service* you use every day?
3. What should you do when someone *has an accident*?
4. How do you *get in touch with* your doctor?
5. Where do you take an *injured* person?
6. How many e-mails or phone calls do you *receive* every day?

COMPREHENSION

UNDERSTANDING THE READING

Circle the letter of the correct answer.

1. Reverend John Flynn _____.
   a. started the Royal Flying Doctor Service
   b. was the first man to visit central and northern Australia
   c. was a doctor who started the Royal Flying Doctor Service
   d. was a doctor who loved to fly

2. The Royal Flying Doctor Service _____.
   a. was not a success in the beginning
   b. helps all people who can afford it
   c. used special radios and airplanes
   d. had no hospitals

3. Outback homes _____.
   a. have special phone numbers
   b. each have their own airplane
   c. have many hospitals nearby
   d. have special first-aid kits

REMEMBERING DETAILS

Reread the passage. Circle **T** *if the sentence is true. Circle* **F** *if the sentence is false.*

1. Flynn traveled for his church all over Australia.   T   F

2. Flynn's first idea was to build hospitals.   T   F

3. Flynn made a radio that could send and receive messages.   T   F

4. Each first-aid kit has the same things in it.   T   F

5. Everything in the kit has a letter of the alphabet on it.   T   F

6. Today, the Royal Flying Doctor Service has twenty-two   T   F
   hospitals.

MAKING INFERENCES

All of the statements below are true. Some of them are stated directly in the reading. Others can be inferred, or guessed, from the reading. Write **S** *for each stated fact. Write* **I** *for each inference.*

_____ 1. Today people use all types of technology to get in touch with the Service.

_____ 2. The Service is still very useful and helps thousands of people every year.

_____ 3. People who know little English can use the first-aid kit.

_____ 4. Everything in the kit has numbers on it, so it is easy to use.

_____ 5. It is very expensive to operate the Service.

TELL THE STORY

Work with a partner or together as a class. Tell the story of the Royal Flying Doctor Service. Use your own words. Your partner or other students can ask questions about the story.

DISCUSSION

Discuss the answers to these questions with your classmates.

1. Would a service like the Royal Flying Doctors work well in your country? Why or why not?

2. What medical services do people need that your country does not have?

3. What can countries do to improve medical services for people who don't live in cities?

CRITICAL THINKING

Work with a partner. Ask each other the following questions. Discuss your answers.

1. Would you like to live in the Outback? Why or why not? What advantages are there to living far from cities? What are the disadvantages?

2. What are some personality traits of people who like to live in remote places? What are some personality traits of people who like to live in cities? What is your ideal place to live?

WRITING

Write six sentences or a short paragraph about the medical service you use.

EXAMPLE: *In my country, when I get sick, I call my doctor for an appointment.*

_____

_____

_____

_____

_____

SPELLING AND PUNCTUATION

CAPITAL LETTERS: DIRECT QUOTATIONS

We begin the first word in a direct quotation with a capital letter. If the quotation is divided into two parts, begin the second part with a small letter. Only use a capital letter for the second part if it is a new sentence.

He said, "**T**here must be some way to help these people. First, I will build hospitals for them."

"There must be some way," he said, "**t**o help these people."

"There must be some way to help these people," he said. "**F**irst, I will build hospitals for them."

A. *Write* **C** *for sentences with the correct capital letters. Rewrite the incorrect sentences.*

_____   **1.** Flynn said, "the doctors can travel by airplane!"

_____

(continued)

_____ 2. His friend asked, "how can they do that?"

_____

_____ 3. Flynn answered, "we will build a place for a plane to land near every Outback home."

_____

_____ 4. "That's impossible," his friend said, "but we can always try."

_____

_____ 5. His friend asked, "how can people so far away ask for a doctor?"

_____

_____ 6. Flynn said, "we will use a radio to send and receive messages."

_____

_____ 7. "Radios can receive messages," his friend said, "but they cannot send them."

_____

_____ 8. The doctor said, "take one pill from number 7 every three hours."

_____

_____ 9. "Put number 16 on your arm," the doctor said, "And take one pill from number 8."

_____

_____ 10. The doctor said, "call me back tomorrow at the same time, and tell me how you feel."

_____

B. _Write two sentences with direct quotations._

_____

_____

 _Go to page 139 for the Internet Activity._

Go to page 139 for the Internet Activity.

| **DID YOU KNOW?** | • When the service began in 1928, the radios they used had pedal-powered generators.
• The flying doctors and nurses are on standby day and night for emergency calls.
• The territory of the Flying Doctor Service covers 2 million square miles, and they can reach any part of it within 2 hours. |  |

WHAT DID THE ANCIENT EGYPTIANS GIVE US?

you read

Answer these questions.

1. Where is Egypt located? What is its climate and geography?

2. What are the ancient Egyptians most famous for?

3. What do pictures of the ancient Egyptians tell us about them?

WHAT DID THE ANCIENT EGYPTIANS GIVE US?

1   The ancient Egyptians gave us many things **related to** buildings, medicine, farming, furniture, metals, clothing, and boats, to name only a few. This **civilization** started about 5,500 years ago and ended about 2,600 years ago. Perhaps one of the most important inventions was the calendar, which organized the year into 365 days and the days into 24 hours. In addition, there are inventions having to do with **communication**, our bodies, and animals.

2   The ancient Egyptians invented many things related to writing and communication. They made paper from papyrus, a kind of plant that grows around the Nile River. In fact, the English word *paper* comes from the word *papyrus.* The Egyptians made pens from plants, and around the same time, they invented black ink. They invented one of the first writing systems, called *hieroglyphics,* which used pictures to represent words. With these **tools**, they made the world's first books about 4,800 years ago. The Egyptians were able to send each other messages **from place to place** over 3,000 years ago by using trained pigeons. This was like the first airmail service.

3   Many things that we wear on our faces and bodies started in ancient Egypt. Both Egyptian men and women wore makeup. The richer they were, the more makeup they wore. Men, women, and even children wore eye makeup. Eye makeup was not only for the rich; poor people wore it, too. The Egyptians believed that by wearing eye makeup they protected themselves against the "Evil Eye." They put the makeup around the eye to make an almond shape. They also liked to wear green eye shadow. Sometimes this **glittered** because it was made from the shiny shells of small insects. They also put a red color on their **cheeks** and lips.

4   Egyptians thought that hair was dirty, so they shaved their heads, and then both men and women wore wigs made of human hair. One Egyptian queen's wig was so heavy that attendants had to help her walk. The Egyptians also invented the first toothbrush and toothpaste. They invented perfumes and deodorants by using flowers and **seeds**. They made the perfumes by mixing these ingredients with oils and fats. The Egyptians were the first to make pins to hold parts of their clothing together. They also used pins to hold up their hair.

5   We all know that the Egyptians built the Pyramids and developed tools to build them. They even made **canals** to transport the building materials to the **building sites**. They used new techniques for surveying and scaffolding. In the pyramids they built, they came up with the idea of tunnels. These tunnels went to underground rooms where they buried the dead.

6   The Egyptians used animals in ways that we do today. The Egyptians loved cats, which were sacred to them, but they also kept them as pets. They also liked dogs, and today's greyhound is a type of dog that began in ancient Egypt. The Egyptians were some of the first people to **raise** bees to get honey. They used honey for their food and medicine. They also made cattle into farm animals and made the donkey work for them. The Egyptians not only controlled animals, they found a way of controlling people. They were the first people to come up with the idea of a police force. Police officers then had much the same job as today!

VOCABULARY

MEANING

Write the correct words in the blanks.

canals	civilization	glittered	seeds
cheeks	communication	raise	tools

1. The Egyptians invented a kind of writing as a form of _____, or a way of exchanging information.
2. The Egyptian _____ started about 5,500 years ago.
3. Egyptians used honey and started to _____ bees to give them honey.
4. The Egyptians had a form of writing, paper, pens, and ink. They had all the _____ for writing.
5. The Egyptians put red makeup on their _____.
6. Some of the green eye shadow they used was very shiny. It _____.
7. They used different parts of a plant, such as the flowers and the _____ to make perfumes.
8. Egyptians used _____, or waterways, to transport material.

WORDS THAT GO TOGETHER

Write the correct words in the blanks.

building sites	from place to place	related to

1. The Egyptians were able to send messages _____.
2. They used different kinds of transport to get materials to the places where they were building, or _____.
3. The Egyptians gave us many things _____, or connected with, writing.

What Did the Ancient Egyptians Give Us?   **45**

USE

Work with a partner to answer the questions. Use complete sentences.

1. What color are your *cheeks*?
2. What form of *communication* do you use most?
3. What is a very useful *tool* to have in the house?
4. What city is famous for its *canals*?
5. What is something people wear that *glitters*?
6. What is a fruit that does not have *seeds*?

COMPREHENSION

UNDERSTANDING THE READING

Circle the letter of the correct answer.

1. The Egyptians made it possible for people to _____.
   a. speak the same language
   b. communicate through written language
   c. draw pictures
   d. send human messengers to foreign lands

2. The Egyptians invented ways to _____.
   a. protect their bodies from injury
   b. decorate and scent their bodies
   c. heal their bodies of disease
   d. make wigs and clothing from animals

3. The Egyptians created the technology for _____.
   a. building homes
   b. laying a system of roads
   c. making canals
   d. burying the dead

REMEMBERING DETAILS

Reread the passage and answer the questions.

1. How did the Egyptian calendar organize the year and day?
2. Where did papyrus grow?
3. What kind of writing system was hieroglyphics?
4. Why did the Egyptians put makeup around their eyes?
5. Why did the Egyptians shave their heads?
6. How did the Egyptians bring materials to building sites?

MAKING INFERENCES

All of the statements below are true. Some of them are stated directly in the reading. Others can be inferred, or guessed, from the reading. Write S for each stated fact. Write I for each inference.

_____ 1. Because the Egyptians learned to write, we know a lot about their civilization.

_____ 2. Wealthier Egyptians wore more makeup than poorer Egyptians.

_____ 3. The Egyptians used perfumes made from flowers and oils.

_____ 4. The Egyptians invented new tools when they built the pyramids.

_____ 5. The Egyptians knew the importance of safety and security in society.

TELL THE STORY

Work with a partner or together as a class. Tell the story of what the Egyptians gave us. Use your own words. Your partner or other students can ask questions about the story.

DISCUSSION

Discuss the answers to these questions with your classmates.

1. What do you know about the ancient people of your country? What is your culture most famous for? What contributions did your people make to the world?

2. Why do today's men and women wear makeup? Why is it so popular? Do you wear makeup? If yes, how much makeup do you wear and why do you like it? If no, why don't you wear makeup?

3. When people learned to control animals, what benefits did it provide to humans? What did it allow us to do? Do you think it's morally right to control animals? Why or why not?

CRITICAL THINKING

Work with a partner. Ask each other the following questions. Discuss your answers.

1. The Egyptians had very distinctive styles of clothing, hair, and makeup. What is the importance of style and fashion in the world today? Is it more important in some cultures than in others? Do you think there is too much emphasis on style and fashion today? Why or why not?

2. In what ways did the Egyptian invention of a writing system change human civilization?

WRITING

Write six sentences or a short paragraph about style and fashion today.

EXAMPLE: *It is important for me to dress in the latest style.*

My friends dress in the latest style, and I want to dress like them.

My style of clothes tells other people about who I am.

_____

_____

_____

_____

_____

_____

SPELLING AND PUNCTUATION

NUMBERS AS WORDS

We usually spell out numbers of one or two words. We use figures for numbers that are more than two words.
> *Their calendar had **365** days in a year.*
> *It also had **twenty-four** hours in a day.*

We spell all numbers that begin a sentence. You can also rewrite the sentence.
> ***Two thousand six hundred** years ago, the civilization ended.*
> *The civilization ended **2,600** years ago.*
> *NOT*
> *2,600 years ago, the civilization ended.*

We spell out the time in words when we use *o'clock*. We use numbers with A.M. or P.M.
> *They got up at **five o'clock**.*
> *His phone rang at **5:15** A.M.*

Exceptions: In technical and business writing, we sometimes use figures. We usually use figures for:
- Dates: *2012*   *July 4, 1776*
- Addresses: *780 Bond Drive*   *402 West 49th Street*
- Money: *$1.25*   *$916.95*

Write C for sentences with the correct numbers. Rewrite the incorrect sentences.

_____ **1.** 4,800 years ago the Egyptians had books.

_____

_____ **2.** There are 80 pyramids still standing in Egypt.

_____

_____ **3.** When I was twenty years old, I went to Egypt and saw the Pyramids.

_____

_____ **4.** 10 days ago, there was an article in the newspaper about a new discovery in ancient Egypt.

_____

_____ **5.** Boys shaved their hair except for one lock until the age of twelve.

_____

_____ **6.** King Khufu had 100,000 men build the Great Pyramid.

_____

_____ **7.** They worked 3 months a year for 20 years.

_____

_____ **8.** The lecture on ancient Egypt starts at 10 o'clock.

_____

_____ **9.** The tour of the pyramid should end by 6:30 P.M.

_____

_____ **10.** Carter discovered Tutankhamen's tomb on November 22, 1922.

_____

Go to page 140 for the Internet Activity.

DID YOU KNOW?

- The Egyptians were the first to celebrate birthdays—but they were only for royalty (pharaohs) and men of high class
- Beer was the most popular drink in ancient Egypt. It was made from bread.
- Ancient Egyptians believed the dead needed food just like the living.

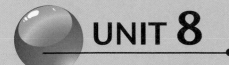

WHY IS LOUIS PASTEUR IMPORTANT?

WHY IS LOUIS PASTEUR IMPORTANT?

1   Louis Pasteur was one of the first people to discover that diseases come from germs. The word *pasteurize,* which we usually see on milk containers, comes from his name.

2   Louis Pasteur was born in 1822 in a small village in France. As a boy, Louis **was interested in** art and was a very good painter. His father did not want his son to be an artist when he grew up. He wanted Louis to be a great teacher. Louis was also interested in chemistry and other **sciences**, so he agreed with his father and decided to go to college.

3   After college, Louis attended a famous school in Paris that trains teachers, the École Normale Supérieure. He entered the school in 1843 to study how to teach chemistry and physics. He soon **made a name for himself** with his research. After he graduated, he became a professor at the University of Strasbourg. At the university, he met Marie Laurent, the daughter of the director of the university. They fell in love and married in 1849. They were very happy and had five children. Sadly, only one boy and one girl lived to be adults.

4   In 1854, Louis took a job at the University of Lille, a city in the north of France. He was a professor of chemistry and dean of the faculty of science—a very high position for a man of thirty-two. Around this time, the French wine industry was in terrible **trouble**. Their wine was **sour**, and they didn't know why. The winemakers around Lille asked Pasteur to help them. After many experiments, Louis discovered that the problem came from germs. The **solution** was to heat the wine. This would kill the **harmful** germs. The winemakers were shocked, but the method worked. Soon they also heated other drinks, such as beer and milk. This made them safe to drink. The method was called *pasteurization,* after Louis Pasteur.

5   In 1857, Pasteur returned to Paris to become director of science studies at the École Normale Supérieure. At that time, there was a terrible disease called anthrax. It killed thousands of sheep and cows every year. Pasteur **noticed** something interesting. If an animal was sick with anthrax and **got well**, it never caught the disease again. He decided to inject healthy sheep with **weak** anthrax germs. These sheep lived and never caught the disease. Pasteur had a vaccine against anthrax!

6   One day in 1885, a doctor brought a nine-year-old boy named Joseph Meister to Pasteur. A mad dog with the disease called rabies bit the boy, and the doctor didn't know how to save him. In the past, Pasteur helped animals with this disease, but would his method work on humans, or would the boy die? Pasteur was very **worried**, but finally he tried an experiment. He injected Joseph with his rabies vaccine and sat by his bed to watch the result. The boy lived! Immediately the news spread around the world, and Pasteur was famous.

(continued)

7   Pasteur wanted to build a research institute in Paris to continue his work. People read about his methods and sent money from all over the world to help build the institute. The Pasteur Institute opened its doors in 1888. It is still one of the world's most respected centers for the study of diseases and how to fight them. Pasteur was the director of the Institute and he worked there until he died in 1895. Everyone remembered Pasteur as a great man.

8   Years later, during World War II, the Germans came to Paris. Some people say that a German officer wanted to open Pasteur's tomb, but the old French guard said no. When the German demanded that he open it or die, the guard killed himself. The name of the guard was Joseph Meister.

VOCABULARY

MEANING

Write the correct words in the blanks.

harmful	sciences	sour	weak
noticed	solution	trouble	worried

1. Louis Pasteur liked art, but he also liked the _____, such as physics and chemistry.

2. When wine becomes bad and people can't drink it, it tastes _____, like vinegar.

3. Pasteur had to find a _____ to the winemakers' problem.

4. The winemakers had problems and needed help. The French wine industry was in

   _____.

5. We can kill _____ germs with heat.

6. Pasteur _____ that if an animal with anthrax becomes healthy, it never catches the disease again.

7. He injected sheep with anthrax germs. These germs were not strong. They were

   _____.

8. Pasteur was _____ about Joseph. The little boy needed help, but Louis didn't want to hurt him.

WORDS THAT GO TOGETHER

Write the correct words in the blanks.

got well	made a name for himself	was interested in

1. Pasteur liked to paint and draw pictures. He _____ art.
2. People began to know about Pasteur because he did important research. Pasteur _____ in the world of science.
3. Animals that were sick with anthrax and _____ never had the disease again.

USE

Work with a partner to answer the questions. Use complete sentences.

1. What is something that is *harmful* to people?
2. What foods or drinks have a *sour* taste? Do you like how they taste?
3. What do you *worry* about?
4. Do you ever feel *weak*? What are some other things that are or can be weak (for example, a sick person, coffee, etc.)?
5. What subjects *are* you *interested in*?
6. When you catch a cold, what do you do to *get well*?

COMPREHENSION

UNDERSTANDING THE READING

Circle the letter of the correct answer.

1. Louis Pasteur discovered _____.
   a. how to make wine and beer
   b. a way to kill harmful germs
   c. how to make a better wine
   d. a way to make wine taste sour

2. Pasteur _____.
   a. invented a vaccine for anthrax and other diseases
   b. invented a method to pasteurize sheep
   c. discovered a new disease
   d. invented vaccines for animals but not humans

(continued)

3. Pasteur's research institute _____.
   a. closed because of World War II
   c. continues to operate today
   b. is a museum today
   d. closed when Pasteur died in 1895

REMEMBERING DETAILS

Reread the passage and fill in the blanks.

1. Marie Laurent was the daughter of the director of the _____.
2. Louis and Marie Pasteur had _____ children.
3. Pasteur's solution was _____ the sour wine. This killed the germs.
4. Before the vaccine, anthrax killed _____ every year.
5. Louis didn't know whether his rabies vaccine worked _____. He was worried, but he gave it to Joseph Meister and waited for the result.
6. The Pasteur Institute is a research center for the study of _____.

MAKING INFERENCES

*All of the statements below are true. Some of them are stated directly in the reading. Others can be inferred, or guessed, from the reading. Write **S** for each stated fact. Write **I** for each inference.*

_____ 1. Pasteur was famous when he was alive.

_____ 2. It worried Pasteur to experiment on Joseph Meister because Pasteur was not a doctor.

_____ 3. Pasteur was not sure that his vaccine would work on humans.

_____ 4. Joseph Meister worked at the Pasteur Institute because he wanted to be near the man who saved his life.

_____ 5. Some people say Joseph Meister killed himself to save Pasteur's tomb.

TELL THE STORY

Work with a partner or together as a class. Tell the story of Louis Pasteur. Use your own words. Your partner or other students can ask questions about the story.

DISCUSSION

Discuss the answers to these questions with your classmates.

1. What scientific discoveries have been made recently?
2. Are all new medical discoveries good? Why or why not?
3. How safe are vaccines and medicines? What about natural remedies, such as herbs and vitamins?

CRITICAL THINKING

Work with a partner. Ask each other the following questions. Discuss your answers.

1. Think about the story of Joseph Meister's death. Why did he kill himself? Do you admire him? Why or why not? Is there anything or anyone you would be willing to give your life for? Name someone who gave up his or her life for something they believed in.
2. Why do you think Pasteur's father didn't want him to become an artist? How can parents' demands help a child? How can they harm a child? Do you think parents should tell their children what to do with their lives? Why or why not?

WRITING

Write six sentences or a short paragraph about a medical discovery that has helped people.

EXAMPLE: *I think antibiotics were a great discovery. Before we had antibiotics many people died.*

_____

_____

_____

_____

_____

_____

SPELLING AND PUNCTUATION

QUESTION MARKS

We use a question mark at the end of a question. The question can be a direct question, a tag question, or a polite request.
- Direct question: *Would the boy die?*
- Tag question: *The story of Louis Pasteur is interesting, isn't it?*
- Polite request: *Could you help me with my report about Louis Pasteur?*

A. *Write C for sentences with the correct punctuation. Rewrite the incorrect sentences.*

_____ **1.** Have you seen a rabid dog.

_____

_____ **2.** Did you know that the word *pasteurization* comes from Pasteur's name.

_____

_____ **3.** Pasteurization is an amazing discovery.

_____

_____ **4.** Do you know that some animals catch anthrax and others do not?

_____

B. *Add the correct end punctuation to the sentences. You can use question marks or periods.*

1. Why was the wine going bad
2. Do you think the medicine would work on humans
3. Could you explain how wine is pasteurized
4. Is it true that Pasteur found the cure for anthrax
5. When people are vaccinated against a disease, they don't catch it
6. Rabies can kill you, can't it
7. They didn't know why the wine was getting sour
8. The Pasteur Institute is in Paris

 *Go to page 140 for the Internet Activity.*

DID YOU KNOW?
- Another Frenchman, René Laennec, invented the stethoscope in 1816.
- A germ theory was put forward by Italian professor Girolamo Fracastoro in 1546, but medicine was not advanced enough to prove the theory or make practical use of it.
- Hundreds of years before Pasteur, the Chinese introduced the first protective vaccination against smallpox.

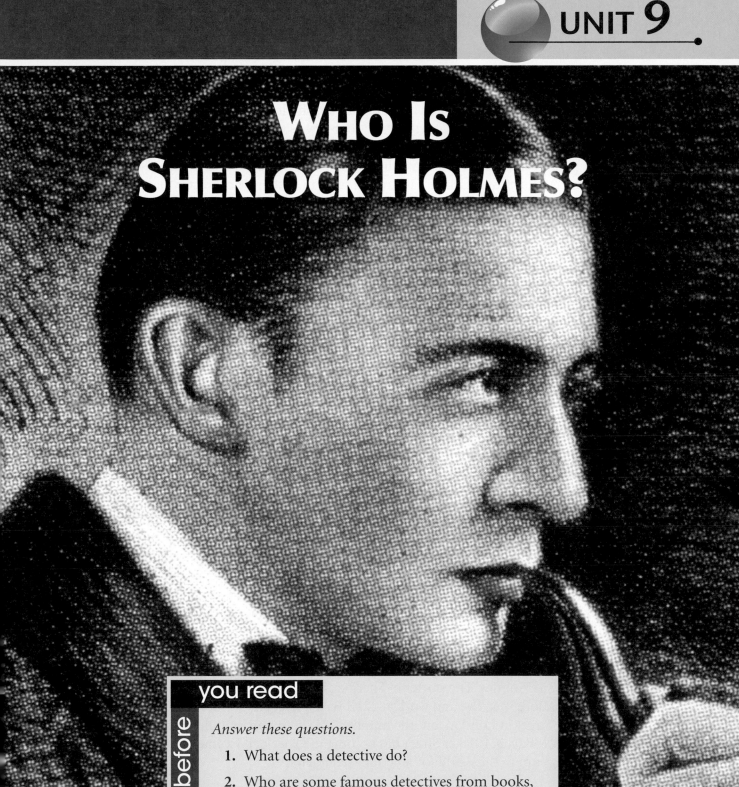

WHO IS SHERLOCK HOLMES?

before you read

Answer these questions.

1. What does a detective do?

2. Who are some famous detectives from books, movies, and television?

3. What are detective stories usually about?

WHO IS SHERLOCK HOLMES?

1   Sherlock Holmes is the most famous detective in English literature. He is the main character in a **series** of stories called *The Adventures of Sherlock Holmes,* written by Sir Arthur Conan Doyle. There are fifty-six Sherlock Holmes stories, published between 1887 and 1927. There are also four novels with Sherlock Holmes as the main character. This extraordinary and brilliant detective is able to **solve** crimes that even the police cannot solve. However, he is a **fictional character** and never existed in reality. Arthur Conan Doyle had created such an **authentic** character that many readers of his stories believed that Sherlock Holmes was a real person.

2   Arthur Conan Doyle was born in 1859 in Edinburgh, Scotland, and became a doctor. In his **spare time**, he wrote books. As the years went by, he became more successful as an author than as a doctor. At age thirty-two, he stopped his work as a doctor and became a full-time writer. The **inspiration** for Sherlock Holmes came from Conan Doyle's teacher at the medical school of Edinburgh University, Dr. Joseph Bell. Conan Doyle remembered how Dr. Bell was able to find out a lot about his patients by looking closely at the smallest **clues**.

3   Conan Doyle did not just write stories and novels about Sherlock Holmes; he wrote other books, too. However, the Sherlock Holmes detective stories became the most popular of his works. At one point, Conan Doyle wanted to do more "important" work, such as writing historical novels, and decided to end the character of Sherlock Holmes. So in 1893, Conan Doyle published the story called *The Final Problem.* Clues in this story suggested that Sherlock Holmes was dead. But the public was very upset. So in 1901, Conan Doyle **had no choice** but to bring Holmes back in the novel *The Hound of the Baskervilles,* which became a sensation.

4   The character of Sherlock Holmes was "born" around 1854. He is tall, dark, and thin. He is intelligent but also eccentric, with unusual eating and sleeping habits. He usually appears cold and **arrogant**. He smokes a pipe and plays the violin. He is famous for solving unusual cases with his extraordinary powers of watching and reasoning. Holmes looks at details carefully and looks for **evidence** at a **crime scene**. He looks at fingerprints, footprints, and even car tire tracks. It is interesting to note that some of the methods used by Holmes were not commonly used by the police at that time. Holmes' friend and assistant is Dr. Watson. He is a short, **stocky** man. Unlike Holmes, Watson is practical. Although Watson is a medical doctor, he is not as clever as Holmes. The stories of Sherlock Holmes are mostly told through Dr. Watson. Both men live and work at 221B Baker Street in London. In real life, there is a Baker Street in London, but the number 221 did not exist at the time the book was written. Today, 221 Baker Street has become the Sherlock Holmes Museum. It is the first museum in the world for a fictional character.

5   There have been plays and movies as well as television series about Sherlock Holmes. Also, there are societies, such as the Sherlock Holmes International Society, which is open to people all over the world. Anyone can join and make friends with other people who are Sherlock Holmes fans. The most famous society is the Baker Street Irregulars. Members meet yearly in New York City for the Sherlock Holmes birthday weekend in January!

VOCABULARY

MEANING

Write the correct words in the blanks.

authentic	clues	inspiration	solve
arrogant	evidence	series	stocky

1. Conan Doyle got the idea, or _____, for the character of Sherlock Holmes from his teacher.

2. The *Adventures of Sherlock Holmes* was not just one book. It was a _____ of stories that came one after another.

3. Sherlock Holmes liked to find the answers. He liked to _____ crimes.

4. Holmes felt he was superior or better than others. He was _____.

5. The character of Sherlock Holmes was so real, or _____, that people thought he was a real person.

6. Sherlock Holmes, just like Dr. Bell, looked at the smallest details, or _____, to help him find answers.

7. He also looked for proof, or _____, such as fingerprints, at the place of the crime.

8. Dr. Watson was short and strongly built. He was _____.

WORDS THAT GO TOGETHER

Write the correct words in the blanks.

crime scene	fictional character	had no choice	spare time

1. In the beginning, Conan Doyle wrote books in his free time, or
   _____.

2. Sherlock Holmes is not a real person. He is a _____.

3. Holmes looks for details at the place where the crime took place, or the
   _____.

4. People were angry when Conan Doyle didn't write any more Sherlock Holmes
   stories. He _____ but to bring Holmes back.

USE

Work with a partner to answer the questions. Use complete sentences.

1. Who is your favorite *fictional character* from a book, movie, or television?
2. What is a famous television *series*?
3. What do you like to do in your *spare time*?
4. What famous person do you think is *arrogant*?
5. How do you *solve* a spelling mistake?
6. What *evidence* would you see if a thief came into your home?

COMPREHENSION

UNDERSTANDING THE READING

Circle the letter of the correct answer.

1. Arthur Conan Doyle had the ability to _____.
   a. make characters that seemed real
   b. fool his readers
   c. write interesting true stories
   d. teach medicine through his writing

2. Conan Doyle made people unhappy when he _____.
   a. didn't finish his last book
   b. killed the character of Sherlock Holmes
   c. wrote a Sherlock Holmes story as a novel
   d. revealed that Sherlock Holmes wasn't a real person

3. Sherlock Holmes solved cases because he _____.

    a. used all the tools the police had   **c.** got other policemen to help him

    b. employed a good assistant   **d.** had the ability to look carefully at things

REMEMBERING DETAILS

Reread the passage and answer the questions.

1. When were the Sherlock Holmes stories published?
2. How was Dr. Joseph Bell like the character of Sherlock Holmes?
3. What other kinds of books did Conan Doyle want to write?
4. What does Sherlock Holmes look like?
5. How is Dr. Watson different from Sherlock Holmes?
6. What is at 221 Baker Street today?

MAKING INFERENCES

*All of the statements below are true. Some of them are stated directly in the reading. Others can be inferred, or guessed, from the reading. Write **S** for each stated fact. Write **I** for each inference.*

_____ **1.** Arthur Conan Doyle preferred to be a writer rather than a doctor.

_____ **2.** People loved the Sherlock Holmes stories so much that they wanted to read more and more of them.

_____ **3.** Sherlock Holmes had some eccentric habits.

_____ **4.** Dr. Watson helped Holmes but did not actually solve the cases.

_____ **5.** Fans of Sherlock Holmes can join the Sherlock Holmes International Society.

TELL THE STORY

Work with a partner or together as a class. Tell the story of Sherlock Holmes. Use your own words. Your partner or other students can ask questions about the story.

DISCUSSION

Discuss the answers to these questions with your classmates.

1. Who is your favorite mystery or crime writer? Why? Who is your favorite detective character from books, movies, or television? Why?
2. Why do you think the character of Sherlock Holmes became so popular?
3. How has solving crimes changed since the days of Arthur Conan Doyle? How was Conan Doyle ahead of his time?

CRITICAL THINKING

Work with a partner. Ask each other the following questions. Discuss your answers.

1. Do you read detective or mystery stories? Why or why not? Why do people like to read or watch detective stories or mysteries?

2. If you had to write a crime or mystery story, what would it be about? What would your detective be like in looks and character?

WRITING

Write six sentences or a short paragraph about your favorite fictional character.

EXAMPLE: *My favorite fictional character is Agatha Christie's Hercule Poirot.*
He is a Belgian detective. He lives in London.
He is a stocky man with a moustache.

_____

_____

_____

_____

_____

_____

SPELLING AND PUNCTUATION

SUFFIXES: -LY

We use the suffix *-ly* to change some adjectives into adverbs.
   *Holmes looks at details careful**ly**.*

We often make spelling changes when we use *-ly*. When we add *-ly* to a word ending in *-le*, we drop the *-le* and add *-ly*.
   *incredible + -ly = incredib**ly***

When we add *-ly* to a word ending in *-y*, we change the *-y* to *-i*, and add *-ly*.
   *happy + -ly = happ**ily***

When we add *-ly* to a word ending in *-c*, we add *-al* before adding *-ly*.
   *basic + -ly = basic**ally***

A. *Circle the correctly spelled word in each group. You may use a dictionary.*

1. comfortably   comfortabley   comfortabily

2. comicly   comically   comicely

3. annualy   annually   annualily
4. sincerly   sincerally   sincerely

B. *Change the underlined words to adverbs by adding **-ly**. Write the new adverbs on the lines. Remember that some words will have spelling changes.*

1. Conan Doyle <u>gradual</u> changed his profession. _____

2. Conan Doyle wrote <u>busy</u>. _____

3. The character of Holmes is <u>authentic</u> portrayed. _____

4. Holmes <u>usual</u> appears cold. _____

5. Holmes' character disappears <u>tragic</u>. _____

6. Conan Doyle brought him back <u>sensible</u>. _____

7. Holmes <u>easy</u> found clues. _____

8. Small clues we <u>typical</u> do not see. _____

9. His methods were not <u>common</u> used by the police _____

   at the time.

10. Members meet <u>annual</u> in New York. _____

C. *Write three new sentences with adverbs ending in **-ly**.*

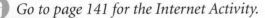
_____

_____

_____

Go to page 141 for the Internet Activity.

Go to page 141 for the Internet Activity.

DID YOU KNOW?	• Sherlock Holmes smokes a pipe in his stories. The pipe we see in movies and plays is different from the one in the stories. The one we see bends downward. This is because the actors found it difficult to speak with a straight pipe in their mouths.	
	• The hat we associate with Sherlock Holmes is not what he wore all the time. The hat called a deerstalker was his hat for the countryside. An American actor, William Gillete, played Holmes in the theater and liked the hat and wore it all through the play. People then started to associate the deerstalker hat with Holmes.	
	• The first movie of Holmes was made in 1906—it was a silent movie.	
	• There are between 200–300 movies about Sherlock Holmes and thousands of television appearances.	

A. COMPREHENSION

Circle the letter of the correct answer.

1. Gutenberg invented _____.
   a. printing with ink
   b. the movable type printing press
   c. printing with metal type
   d. block books printed with wood or metal

2. In traditional African cultures, the purpose of fattening rooms is to make girls _____.
   a. healthy
   b. learn how to become rich
   c. look beautiful
   d. learn how to be good workers

3. The Kumari Devi is _____.
   a. a young girl from a royal family
   b. a young woman with perfect physical beauty
   c. a boy or girl child with blond hair and royal blood
   d. a Sakya girl who meets certain qualities of beauty and character

4. A knight was _____.
   a. a nobleman who fought for the king and lived by a set of rules
   b. any man who had spent most of his life as a soldier
   c. any soldier of royal blood
   d. a wealthy man who helped the king rule the country

5. Roald Amundsen was _____.
   a. the first man to reach the South Pole
   b. the first explorer to reach both the North and South poles
   c. an explorer who died on his way back from the South Pole
   d. the first man to fly an airship over Antarctica

6. The Flying Doctor Service _____.
   a. teaches doctors how to fly small planes
   b. brings patients from faraway places
   c. reaches patients in faraway places
   d. drives people very quickly to local hospitals

7. The ancient Egyptians _____.
   a. grew their hair long to protect themselves
   b. used animals to control people
   c. didn't believe that being clean was healthy
   d. created one of the first systems of writing

8. Louis Pasteur _____.
   a. discovered several new diseases
   b. discovered a way to use germs to create vaccines
   c. invented a way to use human vaccines on animals
   d. invented a way to use wine to fight disease

9. The Sherlock Holmes character is _____.
   a. a brilliant and practical doctor
   b. a criminal who became a policeman
   c. a policeman who is also a writer
   d. an intelligent and eccentric detective

B. VOCABULARY

Complete the definitions. Circle the letter of the correct answer.

1. There weren't many books before the printing press. Books were _____.
   a. huge   b. rare   c. broke   d. over

2. In Niger, women want to be as fat as possible so they eat _____ amounts of food.
   a. slim   b. enough   c. enormous   d. responsible

3. An old Kumari receives a regular payment from the government, or a _____.
   a. pension   b. selection   c. puberty   d. horoscope

4. Queen Elizabeth II of England gives a knighthood to people who have _____ society.
   a. had the   b. contributed to   c. in return   d. doing their duty
   right to

5. Amundsen could not see Scott anywhere. There was _____ Scott.
   a. no sign of   b. no word from   c. had no idea   d. on his way

6. In an accident, a person may be _____, or hurt.
   a. preserved   b. noticed   c. injured   d. satisfied

7. The Egyptians invented hieroglyphics, a kind of writing, as a form of _____.
   a. opportunity   b. tools   c. civilization   d. communication

8. Some germs are _____ and can make you sick.
   a. weak   b. harmful   c. sour   d. tight

9. People who read the stories of Sherlock Holmes thought he was a real person. They thought he was _____ character.
   a. an arrogant   b. an authentic   c. a satisfied   d. a stocky

C. SPELLING AND PUNCTUATION

Circle the letter of the sentence with the correct spelling and punctuation.

1. a. Only the rich new how to read and write.
   b. Only the rich knew how to read and write.
   c. Only the rich knew how to read and right.
   d. Only the rich knew how to wread and write.

2. a. She hopped running would make her slimmer.
   b. She hoped runing would make her slimmer.
   c. She hoped running would make her slimer.
   d. She hoped running would make her slimmer.

3. a. People think their luck will get better if they see the Kumari.
   b. People think thier luck will get better if they see the Kumari.
   c. People think they're luck will get better if they see the Kumari.
   d. People think there luck will get better if they see the Kumari.

4. **a.** Knights protected the week.

   b. Knights protected the weik.

   c. Knights protected the weeck.

   d. Knights protected the weak.

5. **a.** Amundsen was on a boat that went to, Antarctica but he didn't go to the South Pole.

   b. Amundsen was on a boat that went to Antarctica but he didn't go to the South Pole.

   c. Amundsen was on a boat that went to Antarctica but, he didn't go to the South Pole.

   d. Amundsen was on a boat that went to Antarctica, but he didn't go to the South Pole.

6. **a.** "Take one pill from number 8, the doctor said, "and call me in the morning."

   b. "Take one pill from number 8, "the doctor said, "and call me in the morning."

   c. "Take one pill from number 8," the doctor said, "and call me in the morning."

   d. "Take one pill from number 8," the doctor said, And call me in the morning."

7. **a.** The civilization of the ancient Egyptians ended two thousand six hundred years ago.

   b. 2,600 years ago the civilization of the ancient Egyptians ended.

   c. The civilization of the ancient Egyptians ended 2,600 years ago.

   d. The civilization of the ancient Egyptians ended two thousand six-hundred years ago.

8. **a.** Did he know why the wine was getting sour?.

   b. Did he know why the wine was getting sour.

   c. Did he know why the wine was getting sour?

   d. Did he know why the wine was getting sour

9. **a.** Sherlock Holmes carefuly looked at all the details.

   b. Sherlock Holmes carefully looked at all the details.

   c. Sherlock Holmes carfully looked at all the details.

   d. Sherlock Holmes carefuley looked at all the details.

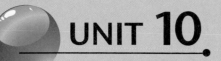

WHAT IS HAPPENING TO THE WORLD'S CLIMATE?

before you read

Answer these questions.

1. What is the weather outside right now?

2. What is the climate where you are living? Is it dry, humid, snowy, rainy?

3. What is the difference between climate and weather?

What Is Happening to the World's Climate?

1   Glaciers around the world are melting. Southern Australia is having **record heat**. Many places are having terrible storms and **floods**. Bees are appearing in Northern Ireland in the winter. What is happening to our climate?

2   Earth has warmed by 1º F over the last 100 years. That may not seem like very much, but even one degree is making great changes on our planet. There is much less ice in the Arctic than years ago. Ice **reflects** the sun's rays and helps keep the Earth cool. Without the ice, Earth would be hotter. Our ocean waters are getting warmer, too. This causes changes in the weather, such as heavy rain in one place and **drought** in another.

3   Changes in Earth's climate are not new. The Earth is 4.6 billion years old. During that time, its climate has **constantly** changed. At one time, the Earth was warm. Oceans covered most of the planet. About 30,000 years ago, huge ice sheets covered much of North America, Europe, and Asia. Over thousands of years, the ice melted. Many plants and animals disappeared. Others took their place. Even in the last 500 years, the climate has changed greatly. There have been cold times and warm times. A "Little Ice Age" started in the fifteenth century in Europe. It lasted several hundred years. Many people died. Others moved to warmer places. In this century, temperatures in Europe have increased more than in most places in the world. There is more rain in the north and less in the south. In Russia, the ground in Siberia is melting. Vast areas that have been frozen for tens of thousands of years are starting to **thaw**. In the Caucasus Mountains of Russia, half of all the ice has disappeared in the past 100 years.

4   Why are scientists **concerned** today? In history, climate changes occurred over thousands of years. However, the eight warmest years on record have all happened since 1998, with the warmest in 2005. That means the Earth is warming very quickly, and you don't have to be a scientist to know that. As glaciers melt, the oceans rise. In Alaska, coastal villages are disappearing under the water. In Kenya, 82 percent of the glacier on Mt. Kilimanjaro has melted. Plants are appearing in the mountains of the western United States where it was too cold for them to grow before. Coral reefs around Australia are dying because ocean waters are getting warmer.

5   Most of us today know about **global warming**. Scientists warn us about it. Politicians argue about it. People everywhere talk about it. Some people say that our climate changes are natural. But most scientists believe that humans are at least partly responsible. In the past, all climate changes were natural. But then about 200 years ago, we started to change the climate, little by little. It started with a period called the Industrial Revolution. It was a time when people began using machines.

(continued)

Factories burned coal and sent heavy smoke into the air. Even today, most of the energy we use to drive our cars, heat our homes, and **run** our **machines** comes from coal and oil. Coal and oil **release** gases into the air. These gases **trap** the sun's energy in the atmosphere. This makes Earth warmer.

6   Is there anything we can do to stop global warming? Well, we can't stop natural changes in climate, of course. But we can certainly make our part in it smaller. There are things we can do to use less energy. We can learn more about our environment, and we can become friends of our planet.

VOCABULARY

MEANING

Write the correct words in the blanks.

concerned	drought	reflects	thaw
constantly	floods	release	trap

1. When there is no rain for a long period of time, there is a _____.

2. When something that is frozen starts to melt, it starts to _____.

3. Our climate is always, or _____, changing.

4. Scientists are worried, or _____, about Earth warming.

5. When a river rises because of too much rain and flows over, it results in

   _____.

6. Earth is getting warmer because gases don't let out, or _____, the sun's energy.

7. Ice is like a mirror. It sends back, or _____, the sun's rays.

8. Fuels, such as coal and oil, send out, or _____, gases into the surrounding air.

WORDS THAT GO TOGETHER

Write the correct words in the blanks.

global warming	record heat	run machines

1. When there is _____, the temperature has never been so high.

2. When you _____, you make them work.

3. The rise of Earth's temperature due to high levels of carbon dioxide and other gases in the atmosphere is called _____.

USE

Work with a partner to answer the questions. Use complete sentences.

1. In which month do you usually have *record heat*?
2. Where do you hear about *global warming*?
3. What is something that *concerns* you?
4. On which continent are there a lot of *droughts*?
5. What is something that is *constantly* changing?
6. Where do people go when there is a *flood*?

COMPREHENSION

UNDERSTANDING THE READING

Circle the letter of the correct answer.

1. Because Earth has warmed by one degree, _____.
   a. ocean temperatures are getting cooler
   b. Arctic ice is melting
   c. there are heavy rains everywhere
   d. less sunlight is reaching our atmosphere

2. Climate changes today are _____.
   a. happening faster than in the past
   b. more extreme than ever before
   c. only a result of natural causes
   d. causing large numbers of plants and animals to disappear

3. Scientists believe that humans have helped global warming by _____.
   a. not using enough energy
   b. burning coal and oil
   c. trapping the sun's rays for energy
   d. using gases to run factories

REMEMBERING DETAILS

Reread the passage and answer the questions.

1. How does ice help keep Earth cool?
2. When did huge ice sheets cover North America?
3. What happened to people during the "Little Ice Age"?
4. Why are coral reefs around Australia dying?
5. What do we call the period when people began to use machines?
6. Where does most of our energy come from to drive our cars and heat our homes?

MAKING INFERENCES

All of the statements below are true. Some of them are stated directly in the reading. Others can be inferred, or guessed, from the reading. Write S for each stated fact. Write I for each inference.

_____ 1. Warmer ocean waters are causing heavy rains in one area and drought in others.

_____ 2. The melting of the ice sheets over North America had a severe affect on nature.

_____ 3. In the future, Siberia will be a very different place than it was a hundred years ago.

_____ 4. Rising sea levels are already affecting the lives of people in coastal areas.

_____ 5. We started to change our climate about 200 years ago.

TELL THE STORY

Work with a partner or together as a class. Tell the story of what is happening to the world's climate. Use your own words. Your partner or other students can ask questions about the story.

DISCUSSION

Discuss the answers to these questions with your classmates.

1. How can climate changes affect peoples' health and lifestyles? In what ways are the effects of global warming appearing in your country? What changes do you think will happen in the future?

2. How important do you think the oceans are to us? How do the oceans affect climate? What do the oceans provide us? How will rising ocean levels and temperatures affect the lives of people around the world?

3. Do you believe humans are responsible for global warming? Why or why not?

CRITICAL THINKING

Work with a partner. Ask each other the following questions. Discuss your answers.

1. Ice is the world's largest supplier of fresh water. It also regulates Earth's temperature. What effects will the melting of ice caps, glaciers, and frozen ground have on people, animals, and plants? Should we be worried about global warming? Why or why not?

2. Is there anything we can do to reduce global warming? What can we do as nations and as individuals? How can the following people help: scientists, politicians, teachers, world leaders?

WRITING

Write six sentences or a short paragraph about what people can do to help stop global warming.

EXAMPLE: *We can ride a bicycle.*

We can bring our own bag when we go to the supermarket.

We can take public transportation when possible.

_____

_____

_____

_____

_____

_____

SPELLING AND PUNCTUATION

CARDINAL NUMBERS AND ORDINAL NUMBERS

Cardinal numbers are regular numbers we use to show quantity.
*Half the ice disappeared in the last **100** years.*

We use ordinal numbers when we want to show where something comes in a series.
In the fifteenth century, there was a "Little Ice Age."

To write ordinal numbers, we put the two last letters of the ordinal number after the number in figures. For example, we can write *first* as **1st**, *thirty-second* as **32nd**, and *fourteenth* as **14th**.

1st	first	9th	ninth	17th	seventeenth
2nd	second	10th	tenth	18th	eighteenth
3rd	third	11th	eleventh	19th	nineteenth
4th	fourth	12th	twelfth	20th	twentieth
5th	fifth	13th	thirteenth	21st	twenty-first
6th	sixth	14th	fourteenth	100th	one hundredth
7th	seventh	15th	fifteenth	1000th	one thousandth
8th	eighth	16th	sixteenth	1,000,000th	one millionth

A. *Rewrite the sentences using ordinal numbers.*

1. We are seeing glaciers melt in the Arctic for the 1 time.

_____

2. This is the 10 time I've read about global warming.

_____

(continued)

3. The Industrial Revolution started in the 18 century.

_____

4. Russia is only the 4 coldest place in the world.

_____

5. Antarctica is the 5 largest continent.

_____

6. He went to Antarctica for the 2 time.

_____

B. *Write three new sentences using ordinal numbers.*

_____

_____

_____

 *Go to page 141 for the Internet Activity.*

Go to page 141 for the Internet Activity.

| **DID YOU KNOW?** | • An average cloud weighs as much as a jumbo jet, but the weight is spread over a large area.
• *Monsoon* is from an Arabic word meaning *season*. The monsoon winds always bring heavy rainfall in Southern Asia in the summer.
• The last 20 years of the 20th century were the hottest in more than 400 years. |  |

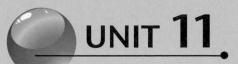

HOW DO KOREANS CELEBRATE A WEDDING?

before

you read

Answer these questions.

1. What gifts do you give for an engagement or a wedding?

2. Do you prefer a modern or a traditional wedding?

3. What do you do after a wedding ceremony?

HOW DO KOREANS CELEBRATE A WEDDING?

1   In the past, parents in Korea arranged marriages for their children. As a rule, they **hired** a matchmaker to help them. A matchmaker was usually a woman in the village. People paid her to find a good **match** for their son or daughter. The couple generally did not meet each other until the day of the wedding. However, arranged marriages are rare today and are more common in rural areas.

2   Today, there are two ways to get married in Korea. The first is by a love match: two people meet, fall in love, and get married. There is no need for a third person. The second way is an arranged marriage: a third person or a matchmaking service chooses two people to marry each other. If the two families agree on the match, the couple visits a fortune teller.

3   Koreans believe in the "four pillars." These are the year, month, day, and hour of a person's birth. A fortune-teller uses these four "pillars" to predict a couple's destiny. Before a couple gets married, the fortune-teller looks at their four pillars to see whether the two people can be happy together. If the four pillars are bad for the couple, the family returns to the matchmaker to try again. If the four pillars are good for the couple, the two can **get engaged**.

4   At the engagement **ceremony**, the two families get together. They can meet at the young woman's house, a hotel, or a restaurant, but never at the young man's house. Today, families usually meet in a restaurant to **set a date** for the wedding. They always give each other lots of gifts. The two young people also **exchange** gifts. Some Korean families spend $30,000 to $40,000 on engagement gifts. One of the gifts to the girl's family is a special **document**. In the middle of a piece of expensive paper, her husband's four pillars are written in ink. The girl keeps this document all her life.

5   The time before the marriage ceremony is very exciting for the boy, called *the groom,* and the girl, called *the bride.* The groom's family sends a box of gifts (called a *hahm*) for the bride. Usually, the gifts are jewelry and some red and blue fabric for a traditional dress. Friends of the groom **deliver** the box at night. They **shout** playfully, "Buy a hahm! Hahm for sale!" The friends wait for the family to give them food and money, then they give the box of gifts to the girl.

6   The day of the wedding arrives! Traditionally, the groom first gives his new mother-**in-law** the gift of a goose. The goose is a symbol of love because a goose takes only one partner in its life. Today, the groom gives a goose made of wood. Then it's time for the ceremony. They have the ceremony at a table. The bride and groom sit at the table. They each have a cup full of a special wine, and they **take a sip**. Then someone takes the cups, mixes the wine together, and pours it into their

cups again. The bride and groom each sip the mixed wine. This is a symbol of their new life together.

7   Korean Americans have a ceremony that is a little different. Family and close friends attend the ceremony. The new wife offers her in-laws gifts of dried fruits and jujubes,[1] which represent children. This is a symbol of her wish to give them grandchildren. Her in-laws offer her tea. At the end of the ceremony, they throw fruit and chestnuts at the bride, and she tries to catch them in her skirt.

8   The wedding **banquet** follows. It is called "the noodle banquet" because there is a lot of noodle soup. As in China, noodles represent a long and happy life. For dessert, there are sweet cakes and a sweet, sticky rice ball. It has chestnuts, jujubes, raisins, and pine nuts. These are all symbols of children.

9   When the eldest son of a family gets married, it is traditional for his parents to move in with him and his new wife. This shows that the son will always take care of his parents, and also that his wife will take care of his parents.

_____

[1] *jujubes:* small, soft fruit candy

VOCABULARY

MEANING

Write the correct words in the blanks.

banquet	deliver	exchange	match
ceremony	document	hired	shout

1. In the past, parents paid a woman to find a bride or groom for their children. They _____ her.

2. The woman tried to find a good _____ for their son or daughter. She looked for two people who were like each other.

3. For the engagement, the families get together and do and say special things. They have a _____.

4. The young woman gives the young man a gift, and the young man gives the young woman a gift. They _____ gifts.

5. The boy gives the girl a special piece of paper, or a _____.

6. Friends of the groom go to the young woman's house and give her a box. They _____ the box to the house.

7. The friends are not quiet. They _____ "Buy a hahm!"

8. There is a special dinner with many people, or a _____, after the wedding ceremony.

WORDS THAT GO TOGETHER

Write the correct words in the blanks.

get engaged	in-law	set a date	take a sip

1. After the bride and groom get married, the groom is related to the bride's mother. She is his mother-_____.

2. The two families decide on a day to have the wedding. They _____ for the wedding.

3. Many couples don't get married immediately. They _____, then wait a while to get married.

4. The bride and the groom drink some of the special wine. They _____.

USE

Work with a partner to answer the questions. Use complete sentences.

1. What famous couple do you think are a good *match*?
2. Do you have a traditional or modern wedding *ceremony* in your country, or both?
3. At what time do people usually *exchange* gifts?
4. What is an important *document* that you have?
5. What is something that people *deliver*?
6. When do you usually *shout*?
7. When do people usually have a *banquet*?

COMPREHENSION

UNDERSTANDING THE READING

Circle the letter of the correct answer.

1. Before Koreans get married, they _____.
   a. go to a fortune-teller
   b. have a banquet
   c. meet at the young man's house
   d. throw fruit

2. At the engagement ceremony, _____.

    a. the young woman's family gives gifts only

    b. the two families meet with the fortune-teller

    c. the two families give each other documents

    d. the two families meet and give gifts

3. At the wedding ceremony, _____.

    a. the bride gets a goose

    b. the mother-in-law gives a goose

    c. the bride and groom sit at a table

    d. the bride gets a box of gifts

REMEMBERING DETAILS

Reread the passage and answer the questions.

1. What are the four pillars?
2. Who predicts the young couple's destiny?
3. What does the young woman keep all her life?
4. When do the friends of the groom deliver the box?
5. Why is the goose a symbol of love?
6. What do noodles represent?

MAKING INFERENCES

All of the statements below are true. Some of them are stated directly in the reading. Others can be inferred, or guessed, from the reading. Write S for each stated fact. Write I for each inference.

_____ 1. The couple can get engaged if the fortune-teller says their four pillars are good.

_____ 2. If the four pillars are not good, the matchmaker has to find another partner.

_____ 3. Parents play an important part when a couple gets married.

_____ 4. It is a custom for the eldest son and his new bride to live with his mother and father.

_____ 5. Today, many Koreans live in cities; in the past, more families lived in villages.

TELL THE STORY

Work with a partner or together as a class. Tell the story of how Koreans celebrate a wedding. Use your own words. Your partner or other students can ask questions about the story.

DISCUSSION

Discuss the answers to these questions with your classmates.

1. Do you think arranged marriages are a good or bad idea? Give reasons.
2. Do you think it is a good idea to see a fortune-teller before a marriage or other important event?
3. Who pays for a wedding and/or an engagement ceremony in your country?

CRITICAL THINKING

Work with a partner. Ask each other the following questions. Discuss your answers.

1. What do you think makes a marriage long and happy? If you were asked to arrange a marriage, what would you look for in the partners?
2. Who takes care of the elders in your culture? Do you think that children have an obligation to care for their parents? How are attitudes about caring for elders changing in the modern world? Are these changes good? Why or why not?

WRITING

Write six sentences or a short paragraph about a wedding or similar ceremony in your country.

EXAMPLE: *My sister had a wedding ceremony in church. She wore a beautiful white dress.*

_____

_____

_____

_____

_____

_____

SPELLING AND PUNCTUATION

COLONS

We use a colon (:) to introduce a list of items at the end of a sentence or to give an explanation.
  - List of items: *Koreans believe in the "four pillars"*: **the year, month, day, and hour of a person's birth.**
  - Explanation: *The first is by love match*: **two people meet, fall in love, and get married.**

We do not use a colon after the words *such as, especially, like,* and *including.*

Put colons in the correct places. Some sentences do not need a colon.

1. They give gifts, such as jewelry, red fabric, and blue fabric.
2. The sweet rice ball has the following raisins, chestnuts, pine nuts, and jujubes.
3. In Korea, there are three kinds of wedding ceremonies Eastern, Western, and a mix of the two.
4. Korea has two parts North Korea and South Korea.
5. An engagement ceremony can take place in any of these places the young woman's house, a hotel, or a restaurant.
6. On the wedding table there are many things, including two candlesticks, chestnuts, and branches of special trees.
7. The second way is an arranged marriage a third person chooses two people to marry each other, and if the two families agree, the next step is to visit the fortune-teller.
8. They hire a matchmaker a woman whom they pay to find a good husband or wife for their daughter or son.
9. The groom's family sends a *hahm* a box of gifts for the bride.
10. The groom gives his mother-in-law a gift of a goose a symbol of love because the goose takes only one partner in its life.

Go to page 141 for the Internet Activity.

DID YOU KNOW?	• In Sweden, there is an old tradition for good luck and prosperity (wealth) in marriage. The mother of the bride gives her daughter a gold coin for her right shoe. The father gives her a silver coin for her left shoe. The bride wears the coins in her shoes on her wedding day. • June is a popular month for weddings in the United States. The month of June is named after Juno, the Roman goddess of love and marriage. • In Germany, friends and family have a pre-wedding party where they throw dishes on the floor and the bride- and groom-to-be have to clean it up. • In Italy, the wedding day is usually on a Sunday, but in the United States, it is usually on a Saturday. • In China, the couple may see a fortune teller to find a suitable wedding day based on the dates when the couple was born.

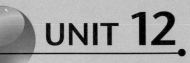

UNIT 12

WHAT IS A MARATHON?

before you read

Answer these questions.

1. What is a marathon race?

2. How and where do you think this race began?

3. Are marathon races held in your country? If so, when and where do they take place?

WHAT IS A MARATHON?

1   It is early morning. A thirty-five-year-old doctor puts on her running shoes. A seventy-year-old **plumber** ties his laces. A nineteen-year-old student puts on her lucky T-shirt. They're all getting ready to run a marathon. Every year, thousands of people **take part in** marathons. They're people of all ages and nationalities. They may be rich or poor. They run along the Great Wall of China and in the streets of Paris. They run in Africa and the Antarctic. The marathon is a great test of **endurance**. But why is it called a *marathon*? Where did it begin?

2   The marathon began with a Greek legend. In 490 B.C.E. the Greeks won a battle with the Persians near the town of Marathon. Meanwhile the people of Athens were waiting anxiously for news. A general in the army asked a young soldier named Pheidippides to carry a message to Athens. Pheidippides ran toward the city, about 25 miles away. He didn't slow down or stop to rest. When he arrived, people gathered around him. Pheidippides gave the news, and then he fell to the ground and died.

3   From then on, the Greeks held a race every year to honor Pheidippides. However, the modern marathon didn't start until 1896. That year the first international Olympic Games were held in Greece. Someone said they should have a race to honor Pheidippides. The race was 24.85 miles long. It started at Marathon Bridge and ended at the Olympic Stadium in Athens. Everyone was excited when a Greek runner won the race, and the modern marathon was born.

4   Today there are more than 800 marathons worldwide. The five largest and most important are in Boston, New York, Chicago, London, and Berlin. The Boston Marathon, which started in 1897, is the oldest. In 1908, the marathon distance was changed for the Olympic Games in London. That was so the race could end in front of the king's viewing box. It is for this reason that today's marathons are 26.2 miles long. In the past, women weren't allowed to race. However, in 1984, the women's marathon became an official Olympic **event**.

5   Marathons are all different. Some run through cities. Others cross mountains. Some are easy; some difficult, and some are quite unusual. There is Norway's Midnight Sun Marathon and China's Great Wall of China Marathon, a Big Five Marathon through big game parks in South Africa and a Polar Circle Marathon in Greenland. The lowest marathon takes place at the Dead Sea in Jordan. The highest is at Base Camp on Mount Everest. The coldest is in Siberia. The hottest is the Marathon des Sables in the Sahara Desert. The temperature goes up to 120° F. It is 150 miles long and takes seven days to complete. Runners carry their supplies on their backs. They need clothes and food. They must also have a **compass, whistle**, knife, and snake venom **kit**!

(continued)

6   Running extreme marathons requires amazing strength and endurance. But it's even difficult for most people to complete a normal marathon. Nevertheless, marathons are extremely popular. Why? There are many reasons why people run marathons. Most don't run to win. Some just want to finish the race. Others want to achieve personal records. Some people **raise money** for **charity**. All want to test their endurance. Marathons **appeal** to people of all ages and backgrounds. But the runners have certain things **in common**—determination to meet a challenge, to run a race, to get to **the finish line**.

Vocabulary

MEANING

Write the correct words in the blanks.

appeal	compass	event	plumber
charity	endurance	kit	whistle

1. A person whose job it is to repair and connect water pipes, is a _____.

2. Some runners need to blow a _____ to make a loud, high sound when they are lost.

3. Runners in the Sahara need to carry a _____ to know which direction to go if they get lost.

4. Marathon runners must have _____, or the ability to run for a long time and not stop.

5. Marathons are liked by, or _____ to, people of all kinds.

6. In one race, runners carry a set of things, or a _____, to use when a snake bites them.

7. The marathon is an _____, or a race, in the Olympics.

8. A runner may collect money for a _____, or an organization that helps poor or sick people.

WORDS THAT GO TOGETHER

Write the correct words in the blanks.

finish line	in common	raise money	take part in

1. Thousands of people participate in, or _____, marathons every year.

2. Many runners collect money, or _____, for an organization that needs it.

3. All the runners want one thing, or they have one thing _____.

4. They are happy when they get to the line that marks the end of the race, or the

   _____.

USE

Work with a partner to answer the questions. Use complete sentences.

1. What *charity* would you give money to?

2. What activity / sport do you like to *take part in*?

3. What do you have *in common* with your best friend?

4. What *event* did you watch on television recently?

5. Where do people usually have a first-aid *kit*?

6. What sport *appeals* to you?

COMPREHENSION

UNDERSTANDING THE READING

Circle the letter of the correct answer.

1. The Greeks held a race every year to _____.

   a. celebrate their victory in a battle with the Persians

   b. remember all the soldiers who died on the battlefield

   c. honor a soldier who carried a message from the battlefield

   d. see who was the best and strongest runner among their soldiers

2. Marathons around the world are _____.
   a. all the same distance
   b. very different
   c. held at the same time of year
   d. mostly held in large cities

3. Most people run marathons to _____.
   a. raise money for charity
   b. become famous winners
   c. meet a personal goal
   d. break the record of other runners

REMEMBERING DETAILS

Reread the passage and answer the questions.

1. Why did Pheidippides run to Athens from Marathon?
2. Who won the marathon in the first international Olympic Games?
3. Where are the five largest marathons held today?
4. When, where, and why was the marathon's distance changed from 24.85 miles to 26.2 miles?
5. Where does the highest marathon take place?
6. What supplies do the runners carry in the Marathon des Sables?

MAKING INFERENCES

All of the statements below are true. Some of them are stated directly in the reading. Others can be inferred, or guessed, from the reading. Write S for each stated fact. Write I for each inference.

_____ 1. It is not only athletes who take part in marathons.

_____ 2. The marathon is a test of endurance for the runners.

_____ 3. Before 1984, woman weren't allowed to run the marathon in the Olympics.

_____ 4. The marathon in the Sahara Desert is certainly the most difficult of all the marathons.

_____ 5. For many people, running a marathon gives them personal satisfaction.

TELL THE STORY

Work with a partner or together as a class. Tell the story of the marathon. Use your own words. Your partner or other students can ask questions about the story.

DISCUSSION

Discuss the answers to these questions with your classmates.

1. Have you ever run a marathon? If yes, why did you do it and would you do it again? If not, would you like to run one? Why or why not?
2. Which marathon race do you think would be the most fun to do? Which would be the hardest? Why? If you had to run one of the marathon races, which would you choose and why?
3. If you could create a course for a marathon race, what would it be and why?

CRITICAL THINKING

Work with a partner. Ask each other the following questions. Discuss your answers.

1. What kind of man was Pheidippides? Was the sacrifice he made worth the price he paid? Why? Is there anything that you would be willing to risk your life for?
2. What are two physical things that you have accomplished—for example, the longest walk you ever took, the highest climb, or the hardest, easiest, hottest, or coldest sports game you ever played? Explain why they were the hardest or longest, etc. Did you enjoy these accomplishments? Why?

WRITING

Write six sentences or a short paragraph about the most difficult / exciting / relaxing sport.

EXAMPLE: *The most exciting sport for me is soccer.*

It is the most popular sport in the world.

David Beckham is the most famous soccer player.

_____

_____

_____

_____

_____

_____

COMPOUND NOUNS WITH NUMBERS

A single adjective made up of two or more words is called a *compound adjective*. The words in a compound adjective are connected by a hyphen or hyphens to show that they are part of the same adjective.

Many compound adjectives have numbers in them.
A thirty-five-year-old doctor puts on his running shoes. (*Thirty-five-year-old* is an adjective that describes *doctor.*)
The doctor went on a 25-mile run. (*25-mile* is an adjective that describes *run.*)

When we use a number in a compound expression, the noun is singular.
Correct: *A three-hour race.*
Incorrect: *A three ~~hours~~ race.*

A. *Rewrite each sentence using a compound noun with hyphen(s).*

1. A boy who is sixteen years old ran.

   _____

2. He ran a race that is 26 miles.

   _____

3. She bought a car that has four doors.

   _____

4. My brother who is ten years old came with me.

   _____

5. We had a training session for ten days.

   _____

6. There was a prize of one thousand dollars.

   _____

7. She can do a run for five hours.

   _____

8. It is a race that is seven days.

   _____

9. You run in temperatures of 100 degrees.

   _____

10. It is a race that is twenty-four hours.

   _____

B. *Write three new sentences about yourself using compound nouns with numbers.*

_____

_____

_____

Go to page 142 for the Internet Activity.

DID YOU KNOW?

- Top men Olympic runners can cover the marathon distance in 2 hours and 10 minutes.
- The world's best long-distance runners who competed for the first time in an Olympic marathon in 1984 covered it in less than 2 hours and 25 minutes.
- The Boston Marathon in the United States, held every year, is the world's oldest and most prestigious marathon, with about 25,000 runners.

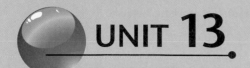

UNIT 13

WHO IS STEPHEN KING?

TERROR

before you read

Answer these questions.

1. Do you like horror movies? Why or why not?

2. What makes you very scared in a movie?

3. What is a famous horror story or book you know?

Who Is Stephen King?

1   Stephen King is one of the world's most famous writers. He has sold more books than any other American writer. His most popular works are horror, or **scary**, stories. But it isn't only his books that are popular. People all over the world **line up** to see the movies made from his books, movies such as *Carrie, The Shining,* and *The Dead Zone.*

2   Stephen King was born in 1947 in Portland, Maine. When he was two, his father **abandoned** the family. His mother had to take care of Stephen and his older brother alone. They moved **from place to place** because it was hard for his mother to find work. It was a difficult time, and they had little money. In the evenings, Stephen's mother read to him. His favorite story was *The Strange Case of Dr. Jekyl and Mr. Hyde.* Later, Stephen read the book himself. He wanted to write a story like it, but he wanted his story to be scarier. Stephen started to write his own stories when he was about seven. His mother always **encouraged** him and sent his stories to publishers. By age eighteen, Stephen published his first story.

3   Stephen graduated from high school in 1966 and **went straight** to college. He studied very hard and always worked in his free time to make extra money. King graduated in 1970. He wanted to be a teacher, but he couldn't find work right away. He had to work at a gas station and then at a laundry service. King finally got a job teaching English at a private high school in Maine. That year Stephen married Tabitha Spruce, his college girlfriend. Tabitha was also a writer. They were happy, but they didn't have much money. They didn't even have a telephone!

4   King started to write a story titled *Carrie,* but he decided no one would like it. So he **threw away** the first pages. Tabitha saw him do it and was upset. She took the pages from the **trash**. She liked the story very much and thought other people would like it, too. She **persuaded** him to finish his book and send it to a publisher. Later, King got a telegram from the publisher. He read it and was shocked. They wanted to publish *Carrie*!

5   At first, bookstores sold only 13,000 copies of the book. Stephen and Tabitha were happy with that, but other people had bigger ideas. The publisher told King he would **earn** $200,000 for the paperback, which sold a million copies in 1975. Soon a company wanted to make a movie from the book, and Stephen agreed. He couldn't believe it.

6   King immediately wanted to buy his wife a **fancy** present. He went to many stores on the way home, but everything was closed except the drugstore. He went in and looked for something nice to give Tabitha, but the drugstore didn't have fancy gifts. He wanted to bring her something, so he bought her a hair dryer.

7   Now that they had money from the book, Stephen and Tabitha didn't have to keep their jobs. They were both going to be full-time writers. Stephen King soon

(continued)

published more books and became rich and famous. He bought a big house in Maine for his wife and three children. It was a house that his wife always liked, but they couldn't afford it until his books became popular. It's an old house with twenty-three bedrooms. Today they live in the same house, and Stephen still works extremely hard. He writes every day of the year except three: Christmas, the Fourth of July, and his birthday. He always writes six pages a day, and he usually works on two different books at the same time.

8   In June of 1999, King was in a bad accident. As he was walking along the road near his house, a van hit him. King had to have three operations on his legs and hip. People thought he might have to stop writing. It took a long time, but King **recovered** and continued with his work **as usual**. Does he ever think he will stop writing? He says he will stop when he can't find more stories—but Stephen King always finds more stories.

Vocabulary

MEANING

Write the correct words in the blanks.

abandoned	encouraged	persuaded	scary
earn	fancy	recovered	trash

1. Stephen King writes stories that make people afraid. They are _____ stories.

2. Stephen's father _____ his wife and children. He left and never came back again.

3. Stephen's mother supported him and told him he was a great writer. She _____ him to keep writing.

4. Stephen did not want the pages anymore, so he threw them out in the _____.

5. Tabitha talked to Stephen and changed his mind. She _____ him to send the book to a publisher.

6. King couldn't believe he would _____ so much money from his book.

7. At first, Stephen bought a simple gift for his wife. Then he paid more money and bought a _____ gift for her.

8. King was very sick after the accident, but after a long time he _____ and was well again.

WORDS THAT GO TOGETHER

Write the correct words in the blanks.

as usual	from place to place	line up	threw away	went straight

1. When there is a good movie, people _____ in front of the theater to see it.

2. Stephen, his brother, and his mother did not stay in one town. They moved _____.

3. After high school, King _____ to college. He didn't do anything in between.

4. King continued to do his work the same way he always did. He did his work _____.

5. King did not want to see his book, so he _____ the book in the trash.

USE

Work with a partner to answer the questions. Use complete sentences.

1. What is the name of a *scary* movie or book you know?
2. When do you go to a *fancy* restaurant?
3. How long does it take to *recover* from a cold?
4. How much does a doctor *earn* in your country?
5. Who *encourages* you to learn English?
6. Where do you usually *line up*?
7. Where do you *go straight* after class?

COMPREHENSION

UNDERSTANDING THE READING

Circle the letter of the correct answer.

1. Stephen King is famous for _____.
   a. writing *The Strange Case of Dr. Jekyl and Mr. Hyde*
   b. writing scary books and movies
   c. publishing a story when he was seven years old
   d. selling more books than any writer in the world

(continued)

2. After the movie *Carrie*, Stephen King _____.

    a. sold a lot of books   **c.** married Tabitha

    b. wrote the book *Carrie*   **d.** threw away the book

3. After the accident, Stephen King _____.

    a. moved from his house   **c.** continued writing

    b. stopped writing   **d.** recovered quickly

REMEMBERING DETAILS

Reread the passage and fill in the blanks.

1. After King graduated in 1970, he worked at a _____, then at a

    _____.

2. His college girlfriend Tabitha was a _____.

3. The paperback of *Carrie* sold _____ copies.

4. He wanted to buy his wife a gift, so he went to the drugstore and bought her a

    _____.

5. King works every day except _____, _____, and

    _____.

6. After the accident, King had to have _____ on his legs and hip.

MAKING INFERENCES

*All of the statements below are true. Some of them are stated directly in the reading. Others can be inferred, or guessed, from the reading. Write **S** for each stated fact. Write **I** for each inference.*

_____ **1.** Money and fame have not changed Stephen King.

_____ **2.** King started to write as a young boy and continues to this day.

_____ **3.** Stephen and Tabitha have a happy marriage.

_____ **4.** Stephen King has liked scary stories since he was a child.

_____ **5.** It is easy for King to find stories to write about.

TELL THE STORY

Work with a partner or together as a class. Tell the story of Stephen King. Use your own words. Your partner or other students can ask questions about the story.

DISCUSSION

Discuss the answers to these questions with your classmates.

1. Why do some people like horror stories?
2. Do you prefer to see a movie or read a book about the same subject?
3. Stephen King is now rich and famous, but he has not changed. Why do some people change when they become rich and famous?

CRITICAL THINKING

Work with a partner. Ask each other the following questions. Discuss your answers.

1. In what ways would your life change if you were rich and famous? How can fame and fortune be a burden as well as a pleasure? Would you like to be rich and famous? Why or why not?
2. Who is your favorite author? What are your favorite kinds of books and movies? If you could write a book, what would it be about? Who would like to read your book?

WRITING

Write six sentences or a short paragraph about a movie you liked.

EXAMPLE: *Last week, I saw a movie about a man who had a special power. He could see things in the future.*

_____

_____

_____

_____

_____

_____

TITLES OF WORKS: ITALICS AND UNDERLINING

Titles of works, such as movies, books, magazines, plays, and television programs need special treatment. When we use a computer, we use *italics*. When we write by hand or use a typewriter, we <u>underline</u>.

Movies, such as *The Shining* and *The Dead Zone* were made from Stephen King's books. (computer)

Movies, such as <u>The Shining</u> and <u>The Dead Zone</u> were made from Stephen King's books. (handwriting and typing)

His favorite book was *The Strange Case of Dr. Jekyl and Mr. Hyde.* (computer)

His favorite book was <u>The Strange Case of Dr. Jekyl and Mr. Hyde</u>. (handwriting and typing)

Underline the titles of works.

1. Have you seen the movie The Silence of the Lambs?

2. King wrote about movies in the book The Horror Writer and the Ten Bears.

3. King's first story was published in Comics Review.

4. King's The Talisman has a story similar to The Lord of the Rings.

5. Mary Wollstonecraft Shelley's Frankenstein is a popular horror story.

6. King has had five of his books on The New York Times Best Seller list at the same time.

7. I saw the movie Carrie with Sissy Spacek.

8. King wrote a TV series called The Golden Years.

Go to page 142 for the Internet Activity.

| DID YOU KNOW? | • Stephen King has had more movie adaptations of his works than any other living author.
• Stephen King has written more than 40 books and 200 short stories.
• King owns three radio stations in Maine.
• King's books have been translated into 33 different languages and published in more than 35 countries. |  |

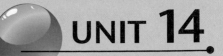
WHAT IS THE STORY BEHIND THE BED?

before you read

Answer these questions.

1. What kind of bed do you like to sleep in?

2. What kinds of beds are there?

3. How do you think people slept a few hundred years ago?

WHAT IS THE STORY BEHIND THE BED?

1   People spend about one-third of their lives asleep. We can survive longer without food than without sleep. Sleeping is very important, so the bed is important. Scientists say that the first bed was probably a pile of leaves or straw. Now, of course, beds are much better than that, and we have lots of **choices**. An average bed today lasts about fifteen years, and most people change beds about five times in their lives. Even with all the beds in the world, people still invent new ones. And some people are still searching for the perfect bed.

2   For most of human history, people slept on layers of cloth, leaves or straw, or furs, which they laid on the floor. In ancient Egypt, over 3,000 years ago, the pharaohs were the first to raise their beds off the floor. They slept on light beds made of wood. You could **fold** and carry these beds. Archaeologists found a bed like this in Tutankhamen's tomb. People back then did not think soft pillows were **necessary**. The Egyptians put their heads on headrests made of wood, and the Chinese had ceramic headrests.

3   In the Roman Empire, only the rich had beds. Poor people still slept on the floor. The bed became a symbol of **wealth**. One Roman emperor had a silver bed. Beds later became a person's most valuable **possession**. When Shakespeare died, he left his second-best bed to his wife. Beds were so special that in England, when a rich person traveled to another person's home, he took his bed with him. When a person stayed at an inn for the night, he had to share a bed with strangers. If a rich person came to the inn, the manager threw a poor traveler out of a bed to make room. All this sharing meant that beds were not very clean, and insects lived in them. Some people, **especially** rich women, slept on a chair when they traveled.

4   After 1750, beds became beautiful pieces of furniture. They were made of carved wood. A beautiful bed at that time could cost $1 million in today's money. The beds had four posts, one on each corner. People used these to hang curtains around the bed. The curtains helped to keep the bed warm. Also, because you passed through one room to get to another, the curtains were good for **privacy**.

5   Beds also became higher and higher. Queen Victoria slept on a bed with seven mattresses on top of each other. She had steps beside the bed to reach the top. Mattresses usually had straw on the inside (for poor people) or feathers (for the rich). After 1820, people slept on cotton mattresses with metal springs inside them. Beds made of metal became popular, too. The best beds were made of a yellow metal called brass. Metal beds were better for your health than beds made of wood, because they had fewer insects in them. That's why hospital beds are metal today.

6   In ancient Rome, people slept in their everyday clothes. In England, people did not wear clothes in bed. They wore a cap to keep their head and ears warm. Later, men wore nightshirts and women wore long nightdresses and hats. **It was only after** 1870 that men started to wear pajamas.

7   People had other interesting ways to **keep warm** in bed. Many families shared one big bed. Some people slept with a small dog to keep their feet warm. Sometimes, people warmed the bed before they got into it. They warmed stones, wrapped them in cloth, and put them in the bed. Later, they used rubber bottles with hot water inside. One English Prime Minister, William Gladstone, filled his bottle with tea **in case** he was thirsty at night.

8   Today, some people in Asian cultures still prefer to sleep on the floor. They sleep on a thick mattress of cloth layers called a *futon*. They can roll up the futon and put it away during the day. Some people put their futon on a low frame rather than on the floor. Then it looks a lot like a Western-style bed.

9   Beds today come in every size and shape. We have round beds, king-size beds, bunk beds, **adjustable** beds, water beds, air beds, and futons. Are you feeling sleepy yet? Sweet dreams!

VOCABULARY

MEANING

Write the correct words in the blanks.

adjustable	especially	necessary	privacy
choices	fold	possession	wealth

1. Today, there are many kinds of beds. We have many _____.

2. In the past, people thought it was not important or _____ to have soft pillows under your head.

3. The pharaohs in Egypt had beds you could bend back, or _____. Then the pharaohs could carry them.

4. Rich people had expensive beds to show their _____.

5. The bed was a valuable _____, or something valuable you owned.

6. Rich people, _____ rich women, did not like to sleep in dirty beds.

7. There are beds today that you can move to any position. They are

   _____.

8. People who did not want others to see them put curtains around their beds for

   _____.

WORDS THAT GO TOGETHER

Write the correct words in the blanks.

in case	it was only after	keep warm

1. People do not want to be cold in bed. They want to _____.
2. Long ago, mattresses were made of straw. _____ 1820 that people used cotton mattresses.
3. Sometimes William Gladstone was thirsty at night, and sometimes he wasn't. He kept tea in his bed _____ he wanted a drink.

USE

Work with a partner to answer the questions. Use complete sentences.

1. What is something in your house that you *fold*?
2. What shows *wealth* today?
3. What is something *necessary* to have in your English class?
4. What is your most valuable *possession*?
5. What do people do for *privacy* in their bedrooms?
6. What do you put on a bed to *keep warm*?
7. What do you keep in your house *in case* the electricity goes out?

COMPREHENSION

UNDERSTANDING THE READING

Circle the letter of the correct answer.

1. In the Roman Empire, the bed was _____.
   - **a.** made of leaves
   - **b.** not important
   - **c.** a symbol of wealth
   - **d.** only in hotels

2. Beds made of metal were _____.
   - **a.** higher
   - **b.** better for your health
   - **c.** more expensive
   - **d.** like beautiful pieces of furniture

3. To keep warm, people _____.

    a. put warm stones in the bed

    b. wrapped their feet in cloth

    c. drank tea in bed

    d. warmed themselves before they got in the bed

REMEMBERING DETAILS

Reread the passage and answer the questions.

1. What kind of headrests did the Egyptians have?
2. To whom did Shakespeare leave his second-best bed?
3. What did people hang around their beds?
4. Why did they do this?
5. How many mattresses did Queen Victoria have on her bed?
6. Why were metal beds better for your health?
7. What do people in some Asian cultures sleep on?

MAKING INFERENCES

*All of the statements below are true. Some of them are stated directly in the reading. Others can be inferred, or guessed, from the reading. Write **S** for each stated fact. Write **I** for each inference.*

_____ 1. Sleep is more important than food.

_____ 2. Manufacturers today don't make beds that last a lifetime because they want to sell more beds.

_____ 3. Beds were not clean in the past.

_____ 4. Asian cultures use a futon because they don't have space for a permanent bed.

_____ 5. In the past, people covered their heads to keep warm in bed.

TELL THE STORY

Work with a partner or together as a class. Tell the story of the bed. Use your own words. Your partner or other students can ask questions about the story.

DISCUSSION

Discuss the answers to these questions with your classmates.

1. What kinds of clothes do people sleep in?
2. Do you think where you sleep affects how well you sleep?
3. What do you know about beds in different countries? For example, some people use pillow-top mattresses, Americans have "king-size" beds, and the French use a *traversin*—a long sausage-type pillow. What do the different beds say about the people?

CRITICAL THINKING

Work with a partner. Ask each other the following questions. Discuss your answers.

1. At one time, beds were a luxury only for the wealthy. Are there differences today between the beds of the rich and poor? What are they? What other luxuries do the wealthy have today? What material things make you happy? What other things make you happy? Which are more important?
2. In spite of our comfortable beds, many people today have insomnia, or difficulty sleeping. Why do you think this is so? Do you think our lives in the modern world contribute to insomnia? Why and how? Do you have insomnia?

WRITING

Write six sentences or a short paragraph about your bed and how you sleep.

EXAMPLE: *I sleep on a bed with a soft mattress. My bed is new and was expensive. I use three pillows under my head.*

_____

_____

_____

_____

_____

_____

COMMAS AFTER PREPOSITIONAL PHRASES

There are different phrases to begin sentences. One type of phrase is a prepositional phrase. A prepositional phrase begins with a preposition (*after, in, on, by, at, for, with, without*). Remember that a phrase does not have a subject and a verb. We use a comma after a prepositional phrase at the beginning of a sentence.

In ancient Egypt, *pharaohs slept on beds.*
After 1820, *people slept on cotton mattresses.*
After a while, *they used bottles with hot water inside.*

Rewrite the sentences with commas in the correct places.

1. After 1750 beds became beautiful.

    _____

2. In England people started to put curtains around the bed.

    _____

3. In fact the kind of curtain you had around the bed showed your wealth.

    _____

4. In the winter people warmed their beds.

    _____

5. On hot nights there were many insects in the bedroom.

    _____

6. By 1900 men started to wear pajamas to bed.

    _____

7. At this time the brass bed became popular.

    _____

8. With brass beds bedrooms had fewer insects.

    _____

9. In Japan people sleep on a futon that they roll up during the day.

    _____

10. At this time there are beds of every size and shape.

    _____

Go to page 143 for the Internet Activity.

DID YOU KNOW?

- In ancient Egypt, beds were not just places to sleep on but were used for eating meals and entertaining socially.
- In 1900, an American furniture manufacturer invented the Murphy bed, which folds up in a closet.
- The air bed was introduced in the 1980s after the water bed, which many found heavy and bulky.

WHAT WERE EARLY PASSENGER FLIGHTS LIKE?

before you read

Answer these questions.

1. Do you think flying is a pleasant way to travel?

2. What do you think airline travel was like 100 years ago?

3. What do you think it will be like 100 years in the future?

WHAT WERE EARLY PASSENGER FLIGHTS LIKE?

1   They were cold, **bumpy**, and dangerous. In the United States, the first passenger airplanes started around 1910 and by 1928, carried about thirteen passengers. Passengers sat down in leather seats that were attached to the floor. These planes had no **air-conditioning** and very little heat. They were hot in the summer and cold in the winter. Because air could not **circulate** in the planes, there was always a bad smell of hot metal and oil. There was also the smell of the **disinfectant** used to clean up after passengers that were **airsick**. The only way to get fresh air was to open the window.

2   Since early planes could not reach high altitudes, there was always **turbulence**, so the flights were very bumpy, and most passengers were airsick. Some passengers wore **helmets** and goggles to protect themselves. Air travel was not a fast way to travel in the early days. Most airplanes could not fly at night because the pilot could not see where he was going, and the plane had to land often to refuel. By the end of the 1920s, it was faster to cross the country by train than by plane.

3   Flying was dangerous and passengers had to be brave. Airlines wanted their passengers to be happy and to come back to fly again. To help them on their flight, airlines employed male **crew members** called *cabin boys, flight companions,* or *flight attendants.* These men were usually in their **teens** and were small and thin. They **loaded** the luggage on the plane, comforted passengers during turbulence, and helped passengers move around the plane.

4   Up to 1930, all flight attendants were men, but this changed. A **registered nurse** named Ellen Church persuaded an airline company that women could work as well as men. She told them that female nurses could take care of sick passengers much better. In this way, nurses became the first female flight attendants. They were called *stewardesses.* They tried to make the passengers more comfortable and offered them water, a sandwich, and even chewing gum to help with air pressure in their ears. They also took the passengers' tickets, carried the baggage, cleaned the cabin after a flight, and even checked the airplane for gasoline leaks. There were strict requirements to become a stewardess. They had to be registered nurses, be no taller than 5 feet 4 inches, and weigh no more than 118 pounds. In addition, they could only be between twenty and twenty-six years old, and had to be single. The requirement of being single continued until the 1960s for most airlines.

5   By the mid-1930s, airplanes could fly higher. They could carry twenty-one passengers and fly from the East Coast to the West Coast of the United States in sixteen hours. This was very fast at that time. With advances in technology, airplanes became better and faster. By the late 1950s, there were more people flying

across the Atlantic Ocean than crossing it on ships. Perhaps in the future, we will be travelling in jets that hold 800 passengers and travel at twice the speed of sound. Flights have come a long way in a hundred years.

VOCABULARY

MEANING

Write the correct words in the blanks.

airsick	circulate	helmets	teens
bumpy	disinfectant	loaded	turbulence

1. Flights were not smooth. They were _____.
2. Passengers were often _____ because the plane was moving up and down.
3. The air in the airplane could not _____ or move about.
4. The cabin boys cleaned up after passengers who were airsick with _____ to kill the bacteria.
5. The plane moved up and down and sideways because of _____.
6. Passengers wore _____ on their heads to protect themselves.
7. The cabin boys were from the ages of thirteen to nineteen. They were in their _____.
8. The cabin boys _____ heavy things, such as baggage, on the plane.

WORDS THAT GO TOGETHER

Write the correct words in the blanks.

air-conditioning	crew members	registered nurse

1. An early female flight attendant had to be officially trained as a nurse. She had to be a _____.
2. Planes were hot in the summer and cold in the winter because there was no _____.
3. Planes had a pilot and _____ to help passengers on the flight.

USE

Work with a partner to answer the questions. Use complete sentences.

1. When do you use *disinfectant*?
2. What time of year do people use *air-conditioning* the most?
3. On what transportation do people wear a *helmet*?
4. What organ in your body *circulates* blood around the body?
5. How can you tell people are *crew members* on a plane or ship?
6. What do passengers have to do when a flight experiences *turbulence*?

COMPREHENSION

UNDERSTANDING THE READING

Circle the letter of the correct answer.

1. Passenger flights in the 1920s were _____.
   a. the fastest way to get from coast to coast
   b. fairly comfortable and enjoyable
   c. usually taken at night
   d. dangerous and unpleasant

2. The first female flight attendants _____.
   a. were certified doctors
   b. helped to fly the plane
   c. had many jobs to do
   d. were strong and tall

3. By the mid-1930s, airplanes _____.
   a. had improved their speed and comfort
   b. still couldn't cross the ocean
   c. were almost as fast as modern airplanes
   d. carried hundreds of passengers

REMEMBERING DETAILS

Reread the passage and answer the questions.

1. What kind of seats did the first passengers have?
2. Why were early flights very bumpy?
3. What were the first male crew members like?
4. Who persuaded an airline company to hire women as flight attendants?
5. What were the requirements to become a stewardess in the 1930s?
6. How fast will jets travel in the future?

MAKING INFERENCES

*All of the statements below are true. Some of them are stated directly in the reading. Others can be inferred, or guessed, from the reading. Write **S** for each stated fact. Write **I** for each inference.*

_____ 1. Airplane passengers in the 1920s were courageous.

_____ 2. By the end of the 1920s, train travel was still faster than air travel.

_____ 3. Airlines hired crew members to keep their passengers happy.

_____ 4. The first female attendants had to be willing to do physical labor as well as nursing.

_____ 5. Plane travel became much more popular in the 1950s.

TELL THE STORY

Work with a partner or together as a class. Tell the story of early passenger flights. Use your own words. Your partner or other students can ask questions about the story.

DISCUSSION

Discuss the answers to these questions with your classmates.

1. What complaints do people have about airline travel today? Do you think they are right? What do you think airlines could do to improve air travel?

2. Would you like to be a flight attendant? Why or why not?

CRITICAL THINKING

Work with a partner. Ask each other the following questions. Discuss your answers.

1. How has airline travel changed the world and the way we live? Was the invention of the airplane good for the world? Why or why not?

2. What are the most pleasant things about air travel? What are the most unpleasant? What are the advantages of travel by air? What are the disadvantages? What is your favorite means of travel? Why?

WRITING

Write six sentences or a short paragraph about what you like or don't like about a form of travel.

EXAMPLE: *I don't like to travel by air because I am afraid in an airplane.*

   I get scared when there is turbulence.

   It takes a long time for me to get to the airport.

_____

_____

_____

_____

_____

_____

SPELLING AND PUNCTUATION

MEASUREMENT WORDS

We use measurement words every day at school, work, and home.
   A nurse had to be no more than 118 pounds.
   She had to be no taller than 5 feet 4 inches.

Here are some U.S. measurement words and their abbreviations. In longer pieces of writing, we usually spell out the measurements. In shorter writing, as well as charts, graphs, and forms, we often abbreviate.

Remember that people in the United States do not usually use the metric system. Sometimes people use it for medical, military, or scientific material.

Units	Abbreviation	Metric Units	Abbreviation
inch	in. *or* "	*meter*	m.
foot	ft. *or* '	*kilometer*	km.
pint	pt.	*liter*	l.
quart	qt.	*gram*	g.
gallon	gal.	*kilogram*	kg.
ounce	oz.	*tonne*	t.
pound	lb.		
ton	tn.		

Here are the words and abbreviations for time measurement.
   hour   hr.   *minute*   min.   *second*   sec.

For sentences with abbreviations, write out the measurement words on the lines. For sentences with measurement words, write the abbreviations on the lines.

1. The flight attendant weighs at least 125 lbs.   _____
2. A Boeing 747 can weigh 435 tns.   _____
3. A flight attendant's minimum height should be 5 feet.   _____
4. Her maximum height should be no more than 6' 2".   _____
5. In the old days, they could gain up to 3 kgs. in weight.   _____
6. It took off in 55 seconds.   _____
7. The flight lasted 16 hrs. and 10 mins.   _____
8. An international plane uses 150,000 liters of fuel.   _____
9. It burns 5 gals. per mile.   _____
10. It travels at 435 kilometers an hour.   _____

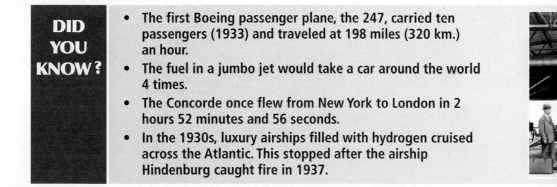 *Go to page 143 for the Internet Activity.*

Go to page 143 for the Internet Activity.

DID YOU KNOW?

- The first Boeing passenger plane, the 247, carried ten passengers (1933) and traveled at 198 miles (320 km.) an hour.
- The fuel in a jumbo jet would take a car around the world 4 times.
- The Concorde once flew from New York to London in 2 hours 52 minutes and 56 seconds.
- In the 1930s, luxury airships filled with hydrogen cruised across the Atlantic. This stopped after the airship Hindenburg caught fire in 1937.

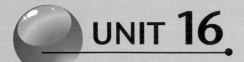

WHO WERE THE AZTECS?

before you read

Answer these questions.

1. Where is Mexico located?

2. What do you know about its history?

3. What do you think an ancient Aztec city looked like?

WHO WERE THE AZTECS?

1   The Aztecs lived in the country we now call Mexico from about 800 years ago. The name *Mexico* comes from the Aztec word *Mexica,* which they used to describe themselves. In the beginning, the Aztecs were a **tribe** of hunters that lived in the north of Mexico. According to a legend, their main god told them to look for a special sign—an eagle eating a snake and sitting on a cactus—and to settle where they found it. Around 1325, the tribe found the sign on a **swampy** island in a lake. They settled there and called it Tenochtitlán. They **drained** the land on the island and built bridges to the mainland. Over time, they added to the size of the island.

2   By 1400, Tenochtitlán was an important city with 200,000 people. The city was divided into four **zones**. Each zone was divided into twenty districts, which were crossed by a network of canals. People used boats to do everyday things. There were three main roads that crossed from the city to the mainland on wooden **bridges** that were removed at night. In the center, there was a **square** with huge temples, palaces, and schools. The city was **symmetrical**, and no construction could be made without the **approval of** a person **in charge of** city planning.

3   The Aztec empire grew and reached across Mexico. It had hundreds of towns and cities and more than 5 million people. Tenochtitlán became the capital of the empire. Most of the people in the empire were not Aztecs, and they had to pay a tax to the emperor. They paid with valuables, such as precious stones or gold. They were punished if they did not pay.

4   The Aztecs treated their ruler like a god. Only the nobles[1] and the priests could talk to him. He lived in a magnificent palace in the center of Tenochtitlán. Aztec society was very organized. It was divided into four groups: nobles, commoners,[2] serfs,[3] and slaves. The nobles helped the emperor rule his empire; the commoners were farmers; the serfs worked on the land owned by nobles, and the slaves were prisoners, usually taken during wars.

5   By looking at the clothes of an Aztec, you could tell how important he or she was. Ordinary people wore plain clothes made of cactus fibers. Only the nobles could wear fine clothes and shoes. Each group could wear certain clothes, and people were punished if they wore clothes belonging to a richer group. Hairstyles also showed a person's place in society. Unmarried women, girls, and boys wore their hair long with **bangs**. Married women twisted their hair on either side to look like horns. Boys who captured an enemy could **trim their hair** to **shoulder length**.

(continued)

---

[1]***nobles:*** people who come from powerful families
[2]***commoners:*** people who do not come from powerful families
[3]***serfs:*** slaves who were sold with the land they worked on

6   In 1521, the Aztec empire ended when the Spanish came to Mexico and took over the region. They destroyed many Aztec buildings and built their own cities and churches in their place. Many Aztec temples are now museums, and the Aztecs don't exist as a tribe today. However, their descendants and other tribes that speak Nahuatl, the Aztec language, number about 1.4 million. Numerous words in English, such as *Mexico, avocado, tomato, chocolate,* and *tamale* come from Nahuatl.

Vocabulary

MEANING

Write the correct words in the blanks.

bangs	drained	swampy	tribe
bridges	square	symmetrical	zones

1. The *Mexica* were a _____ of hunters with a chief.
2. The land on the island was soft and wet, or _____.
3. To be able to build on the island, the water had to be removed, or _____.
4. Tenochtitlán had an open space, or _____, in the middle where there were important buildings.
5. Tenochtitlán was divided into four areas, or _____.
6. The city had _____ that went over the water, but these were removed at night.
7. The two parts of the city were exactly the same; they were _____.
8. Unmarried Aztec women wore their hair with _____ on their foreheads.

WORDS THAT GO TOGETHER

Write the correct words in the blanks.

approval of	in charge of	shoulder length	trim their hair

1. If boys had long hair, they could cut or _____ if they captured an enemy.
2. Boys who were brave wore their hair at _____, or so that it reached their shoulders.

3. There was a special person who was _____ or in control of city planning.

4. All new construction in the city had to have the _____ the city planner.

USE

Work with a partner to answer the questions. Use complete sentences.

1. How often do you *trim your hair*?
2. Who do you need the *approval of* when you want to make a major decision in your life?
3. Who is *in charge of* your classroom?
4. Who do you know (famous or not famous) that has *bangs*?
5. How many time *zones* does your country have?
6. What is the name of a *bridge* you know?

COMPREHENSION

UNDERSTANDING THE READING

Circle the letter of the correct answer.

1. The Aztecs went to the island in the lake to _____.
   a. expand their empire
   b. find water
   c. hunt new animals
   d. settle in a sacred place

2. One hundred years after the Aztecs settled in Tenochtitlán, it was a _____.
   a. small city sinking under the water
   b. medium-sized city with a few buildings
   c. large, well-governed city
   d. huge but disorganized group of cities

3. All the people in Aztec society were _____.
   a. free and equal
   b. ruled by a group of priests
   c. treated harshly
   d. strictly separated by class

REMEMBERING DETAILS

Reread the passage and answer the questions.

1. What sign were the Aztecs looking for?
2. What was in the center of Tenochtitlán?
3. What did people use to pay their taxes?
4. How was Aztec society divided?
5. How did married Aztec women wear their hair?
6. Which Aztec words do Americans still use today?

MAKING INFERENCES

All of the statements below are true. Some of them are stated directly in the reading. Others can be inferred, or guessed, from the reading. Write S for each stated fact. Write I for each inference.

_____ 1. The Aztecs developed an advanced culture in a relatively short period of time.
_____ 2. People who didn't pay their taxes were punished.
_____ 3. The Aztec emperor had great power and control over his empire.
_____ 4. A person's clothing indicated his or her importance.
_____ 5. The Spanish conquered the Aztecs and destroyed many of their buildings.

TELL THE STORY

Work with a partner or together as a class. Tell the story of the Aztecs. Use your own words. Your partner or other students can ask questions about the story.

DISCUSSION

Discuss the answers to these questions with your classmates.

1. What are some of the great ancient empires? Who were they conquered by? What are some reasons why empires eventually fall or decline?

2. In Aztec society, you could tell a person's importance by his or her clothes. In today's world, what are some things that clothes tell us about the person wearing them? What do you think your clothes say about you?

3. What people are you descended from? How much do you know about your ancestry? Is it important to know about our ancestors? Why or why not?

CRITICAL THINKING

Work with a partner. Ask each other the following questions. Discuss your answers.

1. Who are some of the great emperors in history? What empires did they rule? For the people of these empires, what were the advantages of having an emperor? What were the disadvantages? What system of government does your country have? What, in your opinion, is the ideal system of government?

2. Is society in your country or culture divided into groups or classes? If so, what are they? Can people move between these classes, or do they stay in one class all their lives? What class or group do you belong to? Do you wish you belonged to a different class? Why or why not?

WRITING

Write six sentences or a short paragraph about your city.

EXAMPLE: *There is a big square with boulevards that go out from it.*
There are big hotels and several churches in the center of the city.
There is a shopping district in the west of the city.

_____

_____

_____

_____

_____

_____

SPELLING AND PUNCTUATION

COLONS BEFORE LISTS

When we want to introduce a list of items at the end of a sentence, we can use a colon to introduce them. A word, such as *these*, or a phrase, such as *the following* usually comes before the colon.
> *It was divided into four groups as follows: nobles, commoners, serfs, and slaves.*

The sentence before the list should be a complete sentence. If it is not a complete sentence, do not use a colon.

Correct: *In the main square were the city's important buildings: temples, palaces, and schools.*

Incorrect: *It also had: temples, palaces, and schools.*

(continued)

> We do not use a colon after a verb or preposition, such as *in, at,* and *around.*
>> *Among the things the Spanish saw were roads, bridges, and canals.*
>> *There were many people in the market, canals, and streets.*

Add a colon to the following sentences where necessary.

1. The Aztecs grew the following foods corn, tomatoes, and peppers.

2. Ordinary people paid the emperor with feathers, gold, and precious stones.

3. Hairstyles showed a person's status as follows unmarried women and boys wore long hair, married women wore their hair up and twisted in horns, brave boys wore shoulder-length hair.

4. Many Aztec words are used in America today, such as *tomato, chocolate,* and *tamale.*

5. I read about the Aztecs in class, the library, and on the Internet.

6. An Aztec farmer could not do the following go wherever he wanted to, not pay taxes, go out at night.

 *Go to page 143 for the Internet Activity.*

DID YOU KNOW?

- While the rest of the world had wheels, the Aztecs had no knowledge of them.
- The Aztec emperor Montezuma II's headdress, made of feathers and gold, is worth about $50 million.
- Every Aztec boy was trained to fight.
- An Aztec boy became a man after he captured his first prisoner.

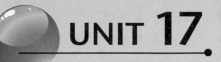
WHERE IS TIMBUKTU?

before **you read**

Answer these questions.

1. Where do you think Timbuktu is?
2. Do you think Timbuktu is a real place?
3. What kind of place do you think it is?

WHERE IS TIMBUKTU?

1   Many people believe Timbuktu is a place of **mystery**. It is a romantic land from **legends**. People often use Timbuktu as a symbol of a place that is far away, unknown, or difficult to reach. For example:

"I want to work in this office, but my company may send me to Timbuktu."

"Sorry I'm late. I had to park my car in Timbuktu!"

"I'm happy that you like your gift. I had to go to Timbuktu to find it."

2   Timbuktu is not only a symbol. It is also a real place. It is a city in the country of Mali in West Africa. Timbuktu is on the **edge** of the Sahara Desert, about eight miles from the Niger River. Even today it is not easy to travel there; the best way to get there is by plane or river. At one time, Timbuktu was a very important city, like Rome, Athens, or Jerusalem. It was the center of learning in Africa, and people called it the "City of Gold."

3   A group of **nomads** created Timbuktu in the twelfth century. By the fourteenth century, it was a center for the gold and salt **trade**. Everyone needed salt, so they charged a high price for it. Sometimes, salt was more expensive than gold! People outside the **region** started to hear and talk about Timbuktu when Mansa Moussa was Mali's king. His religion was Islam, and he built beautiful mosques and huge libraries to spread the religion. Timbuktu was also famous for its universities. The University of Sankore had 25,000 students. People called it the Oxford University of the Sahara. Moussa made Timbuktu into a cultural center for Islam. It became an important city **not just** in Africa, **but also** in the world of Islam.

4   Stories about the wealth of Timbuktu spread **far and wide**, and other kingdoms wanted it for themselves. In 1591, Morocco conquered Timbuktu and controlled it until 1780. During this time, they killed many of the students and teachers, closed the universities, **destroyed** trade, and did not take care of the city. Timbuktu was no longer the City of Gold. After the Moroccans, other African groups controlled the city.

5   In the late eighteenth and early nineteenth centuries, European countries began to make colonies in parts of Africa. Europeans believed Timbuktu was a city covered in gold. They thought gold in Timbuktu was as **common** as sand! Europeans tried to reach Timbuktu again and again, but they weren't successful. They didn't know how to cross the Sahara Desert and survive where it was hot and there was no water. The men died of **thirst** and disease, or thieves killed them.

6   In 1824, The Geographical Society of Paris offered a prize of 10,000 francs to the first Westerner who could **bring back** information about Timbuktu. Many people tried, but René Caillié was the first to reach the city and come back alive. He started on the coast of western Africa and traveled for a year. On the way, he learned to speak

Arabic and dressed as an Arab. He finally arrived in Timbuktu in April 1828, but he couldn't believe his eyes. He saw a city of small houses made of earth—no buildings covered with gold. The economy of Timbuktu was dead, but the intellectual and religious life of the city continued to live. When the French colonized the area some sixty years later, more than twenty schools were still open and were doing very well.

7   Mali became an independent country in 1960. It is a poor country, and Timbuktu is a poor city. Some of the beautiful old buildings are still standing. Sankore University is still open, but today it has only about 15,000 students. In 1974, the government of Mali and UNESCO built a center to hold and preserve over 20,000 old documents from Timbuktu's libraries. These documents were copied by hand over many centuries and contain more than a thousand years of knowledge. It is extremely important to preserve these documents, because Timbuktu is **in danger**. The sand and winds from the Sahara are destroying the plants, the water, and the historic buildings. There is now a program to save the city and its history. People don't want Timbuktu to become only a legend again. Although it is hot, poor, and far away from everything, thousands of visitors come to this city of mystery every year.

VOCABULARY

MEANING

Write the correct words in the blanks.

common	edge	mystery	region	trade
destroyed	legends	nomads	thirst	

1. People don't know much about Timbuktu. It is a place of _____.
2. Timbuktu is a place of unreal stories of the past. It is a place of _____.
3. The city is on the border, or _____, of the desert.
4. People who travel from place to place without a permanent home are _____.
5. People bought and sold gold and salt in Timbuktu. It was a center for the gold and salt _____.
6. The Moroccans damaged and harmed the salt and gold trade in Timbuktu. They _____ trade.
7. Everybody was interested in Timbuktu, including people who lived nearby and people who lived far away from the _____.
8. There was no water in the desert. The men died of _____.
9. There was gold everywhere in Timbuktu. Gold was _____.

WORDS THAT GO TOGETHER

Write the correct words in the blanks.

bring back	far and wide	in danger	not just . . . but also

1. The French gave a prize of 10,000 francs to the person who could go to Timbuktu, return to France, and _____ information.

2. Stories about the gold in Timbuktu went everywhere. The stories went

    _____.

3. Timbuktu is _____ hot, _____ poor.

4. Timbuktu may lose all of its old buildings. It is a bad situation. The city is

    _____.

USE

Work with a partner to answer the questions. Use complete sentences.

1. What is something *common* we use every day in school?
2. What is the best drink for *thirst*?
3. What do people *bring back* from vacation?
4. What television show or movie is a *mystery*?
5. What is the name of a famous *legend* or a person from a legend you know?
6. What *trade* is popular in your country?

COMPREHENSION

UNDERSTANDING THE READING

Circle the letter of the correct answer.

1. Timbuktu _____.

    a. is not a real place

    b. is only a symbol of a faraway place

    c. is a country in Africa

    d. was an important city in the past

2. At one time, Timbuktu _____.

    a. was a cultural center for Islam

    b. controlled Morocco

    c. was made of gold

    d. was easy to travel to

3. Today, Timbuktu is _____.

    a. being destroyed by sand and wind   **c.** a poor city that nobody visits

    b. a colony of the French   **d.** being destroyed by visitors

REMEMBERING DETAILS

Reread the passage and fill in the blanks.

1. Timbuktu is on the edge of _____.
2. People called Timbuktu _____.
3. Mansa Moussa's religion was _____.
4. René Caillié dressed as _____.
5. Mali became an independent country in _____.
6. There is a center to preserve _____.

MAKING INFERENCES

*All of the statements below are true. Some of them are stated directly in the reading. Others can be inferred, or guessed, from the reading. Write **S** for each stated fact. Write **I** for each inference.*

_____ 1. Europeans wanted to colonize Timbuktu, but it was hard to get there.

_____ 2. The Moroccans didn't care about Timbuktu's culture.

_____ 3. At one time, Timbuktu was a rich city.

_____ 4. The University of Sankore was famous.

_____ 5. History is very important to the people of Timbuktu.

TELL THE STORY

Work with a partner or together as a class. Tell your partner the story of Timbuktu. Use your own words. Your partner or other students can ask questions about the story.

DISCUSSION

Discuss the answers to these questions with your classmates.

1. Would you like to visit Timbuktu? Why or why not?
2. What place or city do you dream of visiting one day?
3. What places, such as cities, monuments, or parks, are in danger today? What is being done to help them? What more can be done?

CRITICAL THINKING

Work with a partner. Ask each other the following questions. Discuss your answers.

1. Do invaders always destroy the places they conquer? Most places in the world have a long history of invasion. What are some of the reasons why one country invades another? Is invasion ever right or good?

2. Why is it important to preserve the documents in Timbuktu? Do you think the city should be saved, even though it is poor, dry, and far away? Why or why not? Do you think it's important to save historic buildings in modern cities, or should they be torn down and replaced? Why?

WRITING

Write six sentences or a short paragraph about a place you always wanted to go to.

EXAMPLE: *My dream is to go to Paris one day. I hear stories about Paris. People say it is very romantic.*

_____

_____

_____

_____

_____

_____

SPELLING AND PUNCTUATION

ABBREVIATIONS

An *abbreviation* is a short way to write a word, phrase, or name. We cannot use abbreviations in every kind of writing. Abbreviations are common in advertisements, scientific and technical writing, and other places, such as telephone books.
    The FBI is investigating the crime.

There are several types of abbreviations.

*   one, two, or three letters for a word
    page = p., road = rd., apartment = apt.

*   the first letter of each word, each letter said separately.
    FBI = Federal Bureau of Investigation   *U.K. = United Kingdom*
    UFO = Unidentified Flying Object   *B.A. = Bachelor of Arts (degree)*
    CD = Compact Disc   *M.A. = Master of Arts (degree)*

The recent trend is to write abbreviations without periods, but it is acceptable to write many abbreviations both ways. If you are not sure, check your dictionary.

We may also use the first letter of each word to make a new word called an *acronym*. These words do not use periods.

UNESCO = United Nations Educational, Scientific, and Cultural Organization
TOEFL = Test of English as a Foreign Language
NATO = North Atlantic Treaty Organization
NASA = National Aeronautics and Space Administration

There are many exceptions to these rules. Always check a dictionary or style book if you are not sure of an abbreviation.

Write the abbreviation next to each word. You may use a dictionary.

1. Avenue   _____
2. Mister   _____
3. World War II   _____
4. Boulevard   _____
5. Street   _____
6. miles per hour   _____
7. Medical Doctor   _____
8. Company   _____
9. Doctor   _____
10. Fahrenheit   _____
11. centimeter   _____
12. Automated Teller Machine   _____

Go to page 144 for the Internet Activity.

DID YOU KNOW?
- Timbuktu once had a royal palace.
- The mud mosques of Timbuktu inspired the Spanish architect Antoni Gaudi.
- The population of Timbuktu in 1998 was 31,973.

WHERE DO THE MOST VEGETARIANS LIVE?

before **you read**

Answer these questions.

1. Do you know any vegetarians?
2. What do vegetarians eat?
3. Why are people vegetarians?

WHERE DO THE MOST VEGETARIANS LIVE?

1   Some people choose to be vegetarian, but others are vegetarian because of their religion, their culture, or the place they live. There are vegetarians all over the world, but the country with the most vegetarians is India.

2   About 1 billion people live in India, and most follow the Hindu religion. Hindus think it is wrong to kill or make animals **suffer**. They think if they do, they will suffer the same way **one day**. Hindus believe the cow is **sacred**; therefore, most Hindus do not eat beef. **In fact**, the Hindu word for cow, *aghnaya,* means "not to be killed."

3   There are different kinds of vegetarians in the world. Some vegetarians do not eat red meat, but they eat chicken and fish. Some do not eat red meat, chicken, or fish, but they eat cheese, butter, eggs, milk, and other animal **products**. Other vegetarians do not use anything that **comes from** an animal. Some don't wear wool because it harms sheep, don't use silk because it hurts silkworms, and don't eat honey because they do not want to hurt bees. Other vegetarians only eat vegetables; however they do not kill plants. For example, they will not eat carrots or potatoes because when you take them out of the ground, the plant dies. They will eat apples or pears because picking them does not harm the plant.

4   In India, too, there are different kinds of vegetarians. Some Hindus are **strict** vegetarians. Other Hindus eat all meat, **except for** beef, but they only eat it about once a week. Many families eat chicken or lamb a few times a year at special occasions such as weddings. The Hindus of the upper **classes** do not eat meat or drink alcohol. However, the lower classes eat all meats, except for beef. The upper classes, or *Brahmans,* cannot kill anything that is moving. If they do, they believe they will suffer in the next life.

5   Hindus follow other rules when they eat. They **rinse** their mouths, arms, and legs before and after eating to clean themselves. It is a custom for the man of the house to eat thirty-two mouthfuls at each meal, chewing carefully and thinking about pleasant things. Strict Hindus do not eat garlic or onions. They believe that foods have characteristics. Some foods are "hot," others are "cold." They think the strong smells of these foods are too powerful for the **mild** tastes and smells of other vegetables. Also, in middle-class families, many women do not eat meat, but men do. Women think eating meat is something **masculine**. They also connect meat with **violence**.

6   Hindus also think it is lucky to eat with a person who is 100 years old or a student, but they avoid eating with a bald person, an actor, an athlete, a musician, or a woman with a second husband. Strict Hindus also believe it is not correct for a wife to eat with her husband, but it is good if she eats the rest of his food after he finishes his meal. It is wrong for a Hindu to eat food that has stood overnight, has

(continued)

been cooked twice, or is left over from an earlier meal. Any food that has been touched by a foot, a person's clothing, or a dog cannot be eaten.

7   Vegetarians are everywhere in both rich and poor countries. In parts of the world such as Africa, the Middle East, and Southeast Asia, meat is uncommon, and therefore it is an easy choice to be vegetarian. Surveys show that in both the United States and Britain about 4 percent of the population is vegetarian, and more and more people are choosing vegetarianism every day. Many people become vegetarian for health reasons. They look and feel better when they stop eating meat. Some famous vegetarians include Leonardo da Vinci, Albert Einstein, Thomas Edison, Leo Tolstoy, Brad Pitt, Sylvester Stallone, Paul McCartney, Penelope Cruz, and Madonna.

VOCABULARY

MEANING

Write the correct words in the blanks.

classes	mild	rinse	strict	violence
masculine	products	sacred	suffer	

1. Hindus do not kill cows because they believe cows are very, very special. They believe cows are _____.

2. Hindus believe it is wrong to give pain to an animal and make it _____.

3. Some vegetarians don't eat anything that comes from an animal. They don't even eat animal _____ such as milk, cheese, and butter.

4. It is important for some Hindus to be clean before they eat so they _____ their mouths, arms, and legs with water.

5. Hindu people have different social levels, or _____, from lower to high or upper.

6. Some vegetarians follow all the rules very seriously. They are _____.

7. Some foods have a strong taste; other foods do not have a strong taste. They have a _____ taste.

8. There are special qualities that only men have. These are _____ qualities.

9. When people hurt or kill, they use _____.

WORDS THAT GO TOGETHER

Write the correct words in the blanks.

comes from	except for	in fact	one day

1. A product such as milk _____ the cow.
2. Hindus believe that _____ they will come back to the world as a man or animal.
3. Not all Hindus are strict vegetarians. _____, some eat chicken or lamb a few times a year.
4. Some Hindus eat chicken and lamb. They eat all meat _____ beef.

USE

Work with a partner to answer the questions. Use complete sentences.

1. What are some milk *products* people eat?
2. What is something you usually *rinse*?
3. Is your teacher *strict*, not strict, or very strict?
4. What is a vegetable with a *mild* taste?
5. What movie star looks *masculine*?
6. What do you want to be *one day*?

COMPREHENSION

UNDERSTANDING THE READING

Circle the letter of the correct answer.

1. Vegetarians live _____.
   - a. only in poor countries
   - b. all over the world
   - c. only in religious countries
   - d. only in India, the United States, and Britain

2. Strict Hindu husbands and wives _____.
   - a. never eat together
   - b. always eat the same things
   - c. connect meat with violence
   - d. eat thirty-two mouthfuls at each meal

(continued)

3. All over the world, _____.

    a. people are becoming vegetarian   **c.** vegetarians follow the same rules

    b. vegetarians are religious   **d.** there are more women vegetarians than men vegetarians

REMEMBERING DETAILS

Reread the passage. Circle **T** *if the sentence is true. Circle* **F** *if the sentence is false.*

1.	Some vegetarians do not wear wool.	T	F
2.	Strict vegetarians do not eat potatoes.	T	F
3.	Two percent of Americans are vegetarian.	T	F
4.	It is lucky for a Hindu to eat with a bald person.	T	F
5.	Strict Hindus do not eat onions.	T	F
6.	Rich countries do not have vegetarians.	T	F

MAKING INFERENCES

All of the statements below are true. Some of them are stated directly in the reading. Others can be inferred, or guessed, from the reading. Write **S** *for each stated fact. Write* **I** *for each inference.*

_____ **1.** Many intelligent people choose to be vegetarian.

_____ **2.** Hindus are vegetarian because of their religion.

_____ **3.** Many Americans become vegetarian for health reasons.

_____ **4.** Vegetarianism is growing because meat may cause some illnesses.

_____ **5.** In some parts of the world, people are vegetarian because there is no meat for them to eat.

TELL THE STORY

Work with a partner or together as a class. Tell the story of vegetarians. Use your own words. Your partner or other students can ask questions about the story.

DISCUSSION

Discuss the answers to these questions with your classmates.

1. Do you think it is good for your health to be a vegetarian? Why or why not?
2. What are some rules about food in some religions?
3. Do you think it is right for strict vegetarian parents to raise their children as vegetarians too?

CRITICAL THINKING

Work with a partner. Ask each other the following questions. Discuss your answers.

1. Where, why, and when do you think many of the religious rules about eating, such as not eating meat, came from? Are rules about eating still being made today? What are some examples?
2. What can we learn about people's class, religion, culture, and personality from the food they eat and the way they eat it? What does the food you eat say about you?

WRITING

Write six sentences or a short paragraph about the kinds of foods you eat.

EXAMPLE: *I am not a vegetarian. I eat meat, fish, and animal products because I think they are good for you.*

_____

_____

_____

_____

_____

_____

SPELLING AND PUNCTUATION

SUFFIXES: *-IST, -ER, -OR, -AN,* AND *-IAN*

We add the suffixes *-ist, -er, -or, -an,* or *-ian* to nouns or verbs to describe the person associated with certain things and places.

vegetable	veget**ar**ian	a person who eats vegetables
bake	bak**er**	a person who bakes things
farm	farm**er**	a person who works on a farm

A. *All the people below are vegetarians. Write their jobs on the lines. You may use a dictionary.*

1. Thomas Edison was an _____ (a person who invents things).

2. Marc Anthony is a _____ (a person who sings).

3. Leonardo da Vinci was a _____ (a person who paints).

4. Paul McCartney is a _____ (a person who plays music).

5. Paul McCartney is also a _____ (a person who composes music).

6. Brad Pitt is an _____ (a person who acts).

7. Leo Tolstoy was a _____ (a person who writes books).

8. Albert Einstein was a _____ (person who does work in science).

9. Pythagoras was a _____ (a person who studies mathematics).

10. Yehudi Menuhin was a _____ (a person who plays the violin).

B. *Write three new sentences using the suffixes above.*

_____

_____

_____

 *Go to page 145 for the Internet Activity.*

Go to page 145 for the Internet Activity.

DID YOU KNOW?

- Fruitarianism is a form of vegetarianism where the diet consists of fruit, nuts, seeds and other plants that can be gathered without killing the plant, e.g., if you eat a carrot you kill it.
- Vegetarians and vegans can be overweight too.
- The first vegetarian society was formed in England in 1847 to promote a healthy life without eating meat.

A. COMPREHENSION

Circle the letter of the correct answer.

1. Changes in Earth's climate _____.
   a. have never been as extreme as they are today
   b. are caused mostly by humans
   c. have constantly happened over Earth's history
   d. do not affect plants and animals very much

2. Korean wedding traditions today usually include _____.
   a. giving traditional gifts and having a marriage banquet
   b. seeing a fortune-teller during the marriage ceremony
   c. keeping the bride and groom apart until their wedding day
   d. arranging the marriage using a village matchmaker

3. The marathon race _____.
   a. was first created for the Olympic Games
   b. always takes place in large cities
   c. has always been the same distance and never changes
   d. started in Greece to honor a soldier

4. Stephen King is a _____.
   a. famous author of horror stories
   b. rich and famous movie maker
   c. prize-winning scientist and professor
   d. well-known writer of romantic novels

5. Beds _____.
   a. were not very important to people until modern times
   b. became cleaner and more comfortable over time
   c. were alike for everyone, rich or poor, in most countries
   d. were only used for traveling until the 1800s

(continued)

6. Early passenger flights were _____.

    a. almost as fast and safe as they are today

    b. very safe but not comfortable or pleasant

    c. popular for their speed and level of comfort

    d. slow, dangerous, and uncomfortable

7. Everyone in the Aztec empire _____.

    a. had equal rights and freedoms

    b. was able to move from one level to another in society

    c. lived an ordered life in a strictly organized society

    d. lived in a single group that served the emperor

8. Timbuktu _____.

    a. was a city that existed only in myths and legends

    b. was a poor village that has become a modern city

    c. was a great center of trade, learning, and culture

    d. has always been a poor city of farmers and nomads

9. The one way in which all vegetarians are alike is that they _____.

    a. don't eat meat or drink alcohol

    b. don't eat beef

    c. eat no animal products at all, including milk and cheese

    d. eat only vegetables that do not kill the plant when they are picked

B. VOCABULARY

Complete the definitions. Circle the letter of the correct answer.

1. In many parts of the world, there is no rain for a long time. There is a _____.

    a. flood   b. drought   c. thaw   d. trap

2. In the past, Korean parents did not find a marriage partner for their children themselves. They found a matchmaker and _____ her to do the job.

    a. recognized   b. apologized   c. hired   d. represented

3. Marathon runners have _____ to be able to run for a long time without stopping.

    a. charity   b. endurance   c. appeal   d. kit

4. When Stephen King was a boy, his mother wanted and _____ him to write stories and send them to publishers.
   - **a.** complained
   - **b.** predicted
   - **c.** encouraged
   - **d.** recovered

5. Some people put something to drink near their beds _____ they get thirsty at night.
   - **a.** was a sign of
   - **b.** according to
   - **c.** kind of
   - **d.** in case

6. Early planes moved up and down because of _____.
   - **a.** bumpy
   - **b.** turbulence
   - **c.** airsick
   - **d.** circulate

7. Both sides of the city of Tenochtitlán were the same. They were _____.
   - **a.** symmetrical
   - **b.** zones
   - **c.** square
   - **d.** drained

8. In Timbuktu, there was gold everywhere at one time. Gold was as _____ as sand.
   - **a.** strict
   - **b.** common
   - **c.** strange
   - **d.** scary

9. One Hindu rule is to _____ your mouth, arms, and legs with water before and after you eat.
   - **a.** press
   - **b.** mix
   - **c.** rinse
   - **d.** raise

C. SPELLING AND PUNCTUATION

Circle the letter of the sentence with the correct spelling and punctuation.

1. **a.** Glaciers are melting in the Arctic for first time.
   b. Glaciers are melting in the Arctic for the 1 time.
   c. Glaciers are melting in the Arctic the 1st time.
   d. Glaciers are melting in the Arctic for the first time.

2. **a.** A Korean wedding dessert has three main ingredients: raisins, chestnuts, and pine nuts.
   b. A Korean wedding dessert has three main ingredients raisins, chestnuts, and pine nuts.
   c. A Korean wedding dessert has three main ingredients, raisins, chestnuts, and pine nuts.
   d. A Korean wedding dessert has three main ingredients. Raisins, chestnuts, and pine nuts.

3. **a.** It is a 26-mile race.
   b. It is a 26 mile race.
   c. It is a 26 miles race.
   d. It is a 26 mile-race.

(continued)

4. **a.** Stephen King's books were made into movies, such as "The Shining" and "Carrie."

   b. Stephen King's books were made into movies, such as *The Shining* and *Carrie*.

   c. Stephen King's books were made into movies, such as <u>The Shining</u> and <u>Carrie</u>.

   d. Stephen King's books were made into movies, such as The Shining and Carrie.

5. **a.** In, ancient Rome people went to bed in their day clothes.

   b. In ancient Rome people went to bed, in their day clothes.

   c. In ancient Rome, people went to bed in their day clothes.

   d. In ancient Rome people went to bed in their day clothes.

6. **a.** In 1935, a flight attendant's height could be no more than 5 feet four inches.

   b. In 1935, a flight attendant's height could be no more than 5 feets four inches.

   c. In 1935, a flight attendant's height could be no more than 5 feet 4 inches.

   d. In 1935, a flight attendant's height could be no more than 5 foot four inches.

7. **a.** Aztec society was divided into four groups; Nobles, commoners, serfs, and slaves.

   b. Aztec society was divided into four groups nobles, commoners, serfs, and slaves.

   c. Aztec society was divided into four groups, nobles, commoners, serfs, and slaves.

   d. Aztec society was divided into four groups: nobles, commoners, serfs, and slaves.

8. **a.** People from the u.s. and the u.k. visit Timbuktu.

   b. People from the US and Uk visit Timbuktu.

   c. People from the U.S. and the U.K. visit Timbuktu.

   d. People from the us and the uk visit Timbuktu.

9. **a.** Paul McCartney is a musicist, a singer, a composer, and a vegetarian.

   b. Paul McCartney is a musician, a singer, a composist, and a vegetarian.

   c. Paul McCartney is a musician, a singor, a composer, and a vegetarian.

   d. Paul McCartney is a musician, a singer, a composer, and a vegetarian.

APPENDICES

INTERNET ACTIVITIES

UNIT 1

A. *Work in a small group. Use the Internet to learn more about two of these inventions. Answer the questions. Share your information with your classmates.*

airplane	electric light bulb	reflecting telescope	telephone
compact disk	personal computer	steam engine	

1. Who invented this item?
2. When was it invented?
3. How did the invention change the way people lived?

B. *Use the Internet to learn about two of these inventors who died poor. Answer the questions. Share your information with your classmates.*

Gridley Bryant	Janos Irinyi	Nikola Tesla
Charles Goodyear	Jan Ernst Matzeliger	

1. When did the inventor live?
2. Where did he come from?
3. What did he invent?

UNIT 2

A. *Work in a small group. Use the Internet to find information about health in countries around the world. Answer two of these questions. Share your information with your classmates.*

1. Where do people live the longest?
2. Where do people live the shortest?
3. What country has the most obese (overweight) people?
4. What country has the thinnest people?
5. What are three of the healthiest countries in the world in which to live?
6. Why are the people in these countries so healthy?

B. *Use the Internet to find information on healthy foods. Find five tips (advice) on eating a healthy diet. Then make a list of ten healthy foods. Share your information with your classmates.*

UNIT 3

A. *Work in a small group. Use the Internet to learn more about the Kumari Devi. Answer two of these questions. Share your information with your classmates.*

    1. What goddess is the Kumari Devi believed to embody?
    2. What is the name of the building in which she lives and where is it located?
    3. Who established the tradition of worshipping a girl from the Sakya community?
    4. Where does the Kumari Devi perform her daily rituals?
    5. What does the test for bravery consist of?
    6. What does the Kumari Devi do during the Indra Jatra festival?

B. *Use the Internet to learn more about one of these goddesses. Answer the questions. Share your information with your classmates.*

| Amaterasu | Coatlicue | Freya | Isis |
| Astarte | Diana | Hera | Kali |

    1. What culture worshiped this goddess?
    2. When was she worshiped?
    3. What special powers did she have?

UNIT 4

A. *Work in a small group. Use the Internet to learn about another group of fighters—the Japanese samurai. Answer two of these questions. Share your information with your classmates.*

    1. What does "samurai" mean?
    2. When did the samurai come into existence?
    3. What position did the samurai hold in Japanese society?
    4. What did the samurai learn during their training?
    5. What were the samurai allowed to carry?
    6. What was the samurai code of honor?

B. *Use the Internet to research one of these famous knights. Answer the questions. Share your information with your classmates.*

| Arthur | Gawain | Lancelot | Robert the Bruce | Saladin |
| Don Quixote | Jacques de Molay | Richard Lionheart | St. Martin of Tours | |

    1. Is this knight from history, legend, or a book?
    2. What was the knight's country?

3. When did he live (in reality or legend)?
4. What is he famous for?

UNIT 5

A. *Work in a small group. Use the Internet to research attempts to explore one of these places. Answer the questions. Share your information with your classmates.*

the Amazon rainforest	Mongolia	the Sahara
the Arabian Desert	New Guinea	the source of the Nile River
the jungles of Borneo		

1. Who is famous for exploring this place?
2. When and where did he live?
3. Did he find what he was looking for?
4. What problems did he have?
5. Did he die in the attempt?

B. *Use the Internet to learn about life in Antarctica. Find out (1) who lives there, and (2) what the weather and environment are like. Share your information with your classmates.*

UNIT 6

A. *Work in a small group. Use the Internet to research one of these places where people live far from help. Answer the questions. Share your information with your classmates.*

the Amazon rainforest	the Kalahari Desert	the Sahara
the Gobi Desert	Nunavut	Siberia

1. What country or countries is the region part of?
2. What are conditions like in the region?
3. Who lives there?
4. What kind of communities do they live in?
5. What services do they need?
6. Who provides their services?

B. *Use the Internet to look up one of these humanitarians. Find out when the person lived and what he or she did for humanity. Share your information with your classmates.*

Dame Mary Cook	Gandhi	Florence Nightingale	Mother Teresa
Shirin Ebadi	Nelson Mandela	Albert Schweitzer	Muhammad Yunus

UNIT 7

A. *Work in a small group. Use the Internet to research an ancient civilization from one of these regions. Answer the questions. Share your information with your classmates.*

Central America	the Indus Valley	Iran	Zimbabwe
China	Iraq	Turkey	

1. What was the civilization called?
2. When did the civilization exist?
3. What is it famous for?
4. Why did it disappear?

B. *Use the Internet to look up the ancient civilizations that gave us these contributions. Share your information with your classmates.*

architectural arches	the decimal system of numbers	paved roads
architectural columns	the first laws	the plow
the compass	gunpowder	the western alphabet

UNIT 8

A. *Work in a small group. Use the Internet to research the life of one of these famous people in medicine. Answer the questions. Share your information with your classmates.*

Averroes	Galen	Jonas Salk
Marie Curie	Hippocrates	Andreas Vesalius
Alexander Fleming	Maimonides	Rosalyn Yallow

1. When and where did this person live?
2. What contribution did he or she make to medicine?

B. *Use the Internet to learn about natural remedies. Find and list the natural remedies for each of these problems. Share your information with your classmates.*

backache	cut	heartburn	sore throat
cold	headache	insect bite	

UNIT 9

A. *Work in a small group. Use the Internet to research the famous mystery writer Agatha Christie. Answer the questions. Share your information with your classmates.*

1. When and where was Christie born?
2. How many crime novels did she write in her lifetime?
3. What was Christie's nickname?
4. Who are the two most popular detectives in Christie's novels? Give their names and describe them.

B. *Today, police departments use science to solve crimes. Use the Internet to look up "forensic science." List three ways in which the police use forensic science to solve crimes. Share your information with your classmates.*

UNIT 10

A. *Work in a small group. Use the Internet to discover one way scientists obtain evidence about past or present climate. Share your information with your classmates.*

B. *Use the Internet to research an example of man-made climate change in the 1900s called the "Dust Bowl." Answer the questions. Share your information with your classmates.*

1. When and where did the Dust Bowl happen?
2. What was it like?
3. Who did it affect and how did it affect them?
4. What were the human causes of the Dust Bowl?
5. What did people do to prevent another Dust Bowl?

UNIT 11

A. *Work in a small group. Use the Internet to learn the meaning of one of these wedding customs. Share your information with your classmates.*

cutting a cake	lighting a candle	throwing the bride's bouquet
exchanging wedding rings	throwing rice	wearing white

B. *Use the Internet to research marriage customs in one of these countries. Share your information with your classmates.*

Bangladesh	Greece	Iran	Philippines
Brazil	El Salvador	Nigeria	Saudi Arabia

UNIT 12.

A. *Work in a small group. Use the Internet to research one extreme sport. Answer the questions. Share your information with your classmates.*

1. What makes this sport "extreme?"
2. When and where does it take place?
3. How many people participate?
4. Is there anything dangerous about this sport?

B. *Use the Internet to look up the origins of one of these sports. Describe the sport and say when, where, and how it began. Share your information with your classmates.*

baseball	hang gliding	tepak sakraw	wind surfing
badminton	team handball	water polo	

UNIT 13.

A. *Work in a small group. Use the Internet to find out about one of these writers of horror stories. Answer the questions. Share your information with your classmates.*

Ambrose Bierce	P.G. Lovecraft	Bram Stoker
M.R. James	Edgar Allen Poe	

1. When and where did the writer live?
2. What is a famous story by the author?
3. Is there a famous character from the writer's stories?
4. Have any movies been made from the author's stories?

B. *Use the Internet to research one of these famous modern authors. Answer the questions. Share your information with your classmates.*

Jiro Akagawa	Amit Chaudhuri	Cormac McCarthy	Nora Roberts
John le Carré	John Grisham	Larry McMurtry	

1. When and where was the author born?
2. What type of books is the author famous for?
3. What is a famous book by the author?
4. Have any movies been made from the author's books?

UNIT 14.

A. *Work in a small group. Use the Internet to research different kinds of beds. Make a list of five bed types and describe each. Decide which type is your group's favorite and why. Share your information with your classmates.*

B. *Use the Internet to find out what happens when people don't get enough sleep. Also, find tips on how to sleep better. List five problems that can result from lack of sleep. Then list five tips on how to sleep better at night. Share your information with your classmates.*

UNIT 15.

A. *Work in a small group. Use the Internet to learn about one of these people from the early history of flight. Answer the questions. Share your information with your classmates.*

Juan de la Cierva	Henri Fabre	Harriet Quimby	Charles Kingsford Smith
Amelia Earhart	Charles Lindbergh	Helen Richey	

1. When and where did the person live?
2. What did he or she do that was special?
3. How did the person die?

B. *Use the Internet to research the history of one of these means of travel. Find out what travel was like for passengers in the early days. Share your information with your classmates.*

automobile	ship	subway (metro)	train

UNIT 16.

A. *Work in a small group. Use the Internet to research one of these Native American groups. Answer the questions. Share your information with your classmates.*

Hopi	Iroquois	Olmec	Sioux
Inuit	Maya	Seminole	Zapotec

1. When and where did these people live?
2. How did they live (by growing crops, hunting, etc.)?
3. Did they have any famous leaders?
4. Did they have trouble with Europeans?
5. Do they still exist today?

(continued)

B. *Use the Internet to learn more about the Aztec civilization. Find the answers to two of these questions. Share your information with your classmates.*

1. What was the main crop planted by the Aztecs?
2. How did the Aztecs grow food on their swampy island?
3. What was the position of women in Aztec society?
4. How did the upper class decorate their clothing?
5. What did the Sun Stone calendar represent?
6. What was the main reason Cortéz wanted to conquer the Aztecs?
7. What city is built on the ruins of Tenochtitlán?

UNIT 17.

A. *Work in a small group. Use the Internet to learn about one of these UNESCO World Heritage Sites. Answer the questions. Share your information with your classmates.*

Aksum	Great Zimbabwe National Monument	Surtsey
Butrint	Iguazu National Park	Taxila
the Great Barrier Reef	the Old City of Dubrovnik	Timgad

1. What is a UNESCO World Heritage Site?
2. What is the purpose of the World Heritage program?
3. What is the site you researched?
4. Where is it?
5. Why is it important?

B. *Use the Internet to research one of these famous places. Answer the questions. Share your information with your classmates.*

Camelot	Cibola	Harappa	Mycenae	Troy
Carthage	El Dorado	the Lost City of Z	Shangri-la	

1. Is the place real or legendary?
2. Why is it famous?
3. If the place is real, when and where did it exist?
4. If it is not real, what stories were told about it?
5. Is there a famous person connected with the place?
6. Is there a famous book about the place?
7. Did a famous person try to find the place?

UNIT 18

A. *Work in a small group. Use the Internet to research rules about food and drink in one of these religions. Share your information with your classmates.*

Buddhism	Islam	Mormonism
Eastern Orthodox Christianity	Judaism	Roman Catholicism

B. *Use the Internet to research healthy foods for the mind and body. Find a healthy food beneficial to three of these. Share your information with your classmates.*

bones	depression	hair	high blood pressure	nails
brain	eyes	heart	muscles	skin

MAP OF THE WORLD

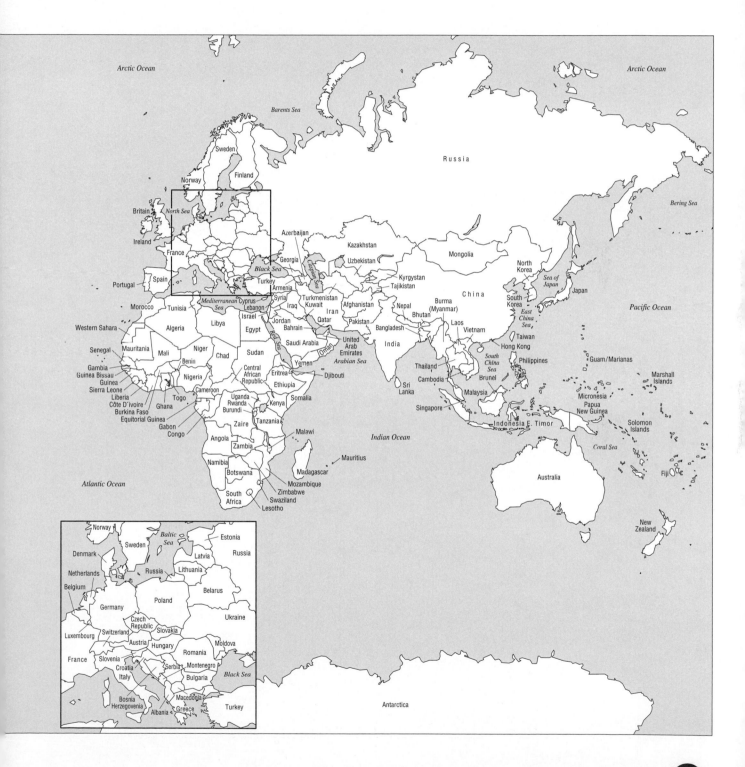

Arctic Ocean

Arctic Ocean

Barents Sea

Bering Sea

Sweden

Russia

Norway   Finland

Britain   North Sea

Ireland   Azerbaijan

France   Georgia   Kazakhstan   Mongolia   North Korea

Portugal   Spain   Black Sea   Uzbekistan   Sea of Japan   Japan

Turkey   Armenia   Kyrgystan   South Korea

Morocco   Tunisia   Mediterranean Sea   Cyprus   Syria   Iraq   Turkmenistan   Tajikistan   China   East China Sea   Pacific Ocean

Lebanon   Kuwait   Afghanistan   Burma (Myanmar)

Western Sahara   Algeria   Libya   Israel   Jordan   Bahrain   Iran   Pakistan   Nepal   Bhutan   Laos   Taiwan

Egypt   Qatar   United Arab Emirates   India   Bangladesh   Vietnam   Hong Kong

Senegal   Mauritania   Niger   Sudan   Saudi Arabia   Oman   Arabian Sea   Thailand   South China Sea   Philippines   Guam/Marianas

Gambia   Mali   Yemen   Sri Lanka   Cambodia   Brunel   Marshall Islands

Guinea Bissau   Chad   Central African Republic   Eritrea   Djibouti   Malaysia   Micronesia

Guinea   Nigeria   Ethiopia   Somalia   Singapore   Papua New Guinea

Sierra Leone   Indonesia E. Timor   Solomon Islands

Liberia   Cameroon   Uganda   Kenya

Côte D'ivoire   Togo   Ghana   Rwanda   Burundi

Burkina Faso   Zaire   Tanzania   Coral Sea

Equitorial Guinea   Malawi

Gabon   Congo   Angola   Zambia   Madagascar   Indian Ocean   Australia   Fiji

Namibia   Botswana   Mauritius

Atlantic Ocean   South Africa   Zimbabwe   Mozambique   New Zealand

Swaziland

Lesotho

Norway   Baltic Sea

Denmark   Sweden   Estonia   Russia

Netherlands   Russia   Latvia

Belgium   Lithuania

Germany   Poland   Belarus

Luxembourg   Czech Republic   Slovakia   Ukraine

Switzerland   Austria   Hungary   Moldova

France   Slovenia   Romania   Black Sea

Croatia   Serbia   Montenegro   Antarctica

Italy   Bulgaria

Bosnia   Macedonia

Herzegovina   Albania   Greece   Turkey